About Island Press

Since 1984, the nonprofit organization Island Press has been stimulating, shaping, and communicating ideas that are essential for solving environmental problems worldwide. With more than 1,000 titles in print and some 30 new releases each year, we are the nation's leading publisher on environmental issues. We identify innovative thinkers and emerging trends in the environmental field. We work with world-renowned experts and authors to develop cross-disciplinary solutions to environmental challenges.

Island Press designs and executes educational campaigns, in conjunction with our authors, to communicate their critical messages in print, in person, and online using the latest technologies, innovative programs, and the media. Our goal is to reach targeted audiences—scientists, policy makers, environmental advocates, urban planners, the media, and concerned citizens—with information that can be used to create the framework for long-term ecological health and human well-being.

Island Press gratefully acknowledges major support from The Bobolink Foundation, Caldera Foundation, The Curtis and Edith Munson Foundation, The Forrest C. and Frances H. Lattner Foundation, The JPB Foundation, The Kresge Foundation, The Summit Charitable Foundation, Inc., and many other generous organizations and individuals.

Generous support for this publication was provided by Margot and John Ernst.

The opinions expressed in this book are those of the author(s) and do not necessarily reflect the views of our supporters.

Bird Brother

Bird Brother

A FALCONER'S JOURNEY
AND THE HEALING POWER OF WILDLIFE

Rodney Stotts with Kate Pipkin

ISLANDPRESS | Washington | Covelo

Library of Congress Control Number: 2021939614

All Island Press books are printed on environmentally responsible materials.

Manufactured in the United States of America
10 9 8 7 6 5 4 3 2

Keywords: Anacostia River, bald eagle reintroduction, conservation, Dippy's Dream, Earth Conservation Corps, environmental education, Falconer, falconry, hawk, nature therapy, raptor, raptor rehabilitation, Rodney's Raptors, Washington, DC

To my mom, Mary (Dippy), and my brother,
Charles (Chuck), who helped make me the man
I am today. My love forever.

Contents

Chapter 1

I sat on the couch, lit a cigarette, and waited for T to come in from the back room with my eightball of cocaine. The smell of sulfur from the match still tickled my nostrils as I pulled on the cigarette. The first drag is always the best. The way it fills your lungs with a warmth that spreads through your body and seems to give your mind everything it needs. I knew I needed to quit, but not today.

Although the room was air-conditioned, I leaned back and wiped my forehead with the back of my hand, still recovering from the suffocating mid-August heat and humidity of Southeast Washington, DC. T had offered me a gin and tonic before he left the room, but I would have preferred an icy glass of really sweet tea. Maybe I would make some when I got home. I've never really had a taste for alcohol except for the occasional beer, and of course I never broke the number-one rule of any smart drug dealer: Do not use your product. Ever. But sugar and sweet drinks? Those were my addictions. And cigarettes. And dealing dope.

T had a nice apartment. I was pretty sure he didn't live there, just kept it as a meeting place, but that wasn't my business anyway. My 9mm pistol was poking into my back, but I didn't want to take it out and put it on the table. T knew I was armed but a move like that could be misunderstood as some sort of threat.

The relationship between two drug dealers and their transactions has to be carefully navigated and controlled. Say the wrong thing, make the wrong move, and you might get a mark put on your back. My MO was to stay calm and relaxed but alert—always looking around, like a hawk.

"Okay, Rodney, let's get down to business," T said as he came back to the room with a broad smile and sat down across from me in a director's chair with shiny metal arms. He put a plastic bag and a triple beam scale on the table between us. At that time—1992—digital scales weren't around much, but the triple beam gave a precise measurement.

"What happened to your hand, man?" T asked, pointing to the bandage wrapped around my left hand.

"Drive-by," I said. "I was seeing this girl down at Condon Terrace, and you know how it goes: some idiot with a gun, pissed at one person but shooting at everybody."

"You go to the hospital?"

T and I looked at each other and we both busted out laughing at the joke. Everybody knows that if you go to the hospital with a gunshot wound, the cops are gonna be called. Unless you're about to die, you don't go.

"It's not that bad," I said. "The bullet went clean through my hand so there wasn't even much blood." It had hurt like hell, but I didn't admit that to T.

"Dang, Dog, Condon Terrace projects, that's a danger zone, all right."

My nickname at the time was Dog, because I had pit bulls. They were my pets, and I loved them like my children. But I had also trained them well, so they served a double purpose of keeping people at a distance.

T and I talked for a few more minutes about the perils of drive-by shootings, which were practically a daily occurrence in Southeast DC, and then T said, "Okay, let's do this." He was a serious businessman and didn't like wasting his time. Neither did I.

He used a small spoon to measure out the white powder and gestured for me to sample. I put my pinky finger on my tongue and then gently dipped it in the coke. I rubbed the powder along the gums above my upper teeth and then on the gums of my lower jaw until I felt the familiar tingle and numbness.

"Oh yeah, that's good," I said.

"I aim to please," T said with a laugh.

Just as T started to spoon the coke onto the scale, a large shadow passed by the side window.

"What was that?" I said, standing up and walking over to the window. T ignored me, focused on measuring the coke.

The window looked out on an empty overgrown lot strewn with empty bottles and crumpled fast-food bags. Then I saw it, on the edge of the roof of an abandoned house next door, just about ten yards away—a huge hawk, with a rodent dangling from its white, curved beak. The bird tilted its head and looked at me with intense golden eyes. This creature was impressive.

I didn't know it at the time, but I was looking at a red-tailed hawk, one of the most common hawks in North America. I had always been fascinated by birds, especially the big ones like hawks, owls, falcons, eagles, and vultures. The first large bird I ever saw was a bald eagle. I must have been in the third or fourth grade, and our class went on a trip to the National Zoo on Connecticut Avenue in Woodley Park. The wingspan of that eagle was close to eight feet. Its curved yellow beak was a deadly hook from which almost nothing would escape death. The white feathers on its head rippled across the tops of his eyes, making him look proud and defiant. For a kid like me from the DC housing projects, this was mesmerizing. And so began my obsession with raptors. They were fierce. They were deadly. They were respected. That's what I aimed to be. And now, with my guns and dogs, I was.

It wasn't just large birds that fascinated me as a child. From the beginning, animals and curiosity about them were a major part of my life. Even growing up in the dirty, violent streets of Southeast, a connection to nature always ran through my body, as natural as the blood in my veins. If I had to guess, I'd say it came from my mom's side. Her grandmother had a farm in Falls Church, Virginia. Cows, pigs, chickens, ducks, you name it, it was on my great-granny's farm.

Sometimes Mom would take us there on weekends. The smell of hay, manure, fresh earth, and animal made me laugh out loud. I don't know why—it just made me so happy. Whenever we went to the farm, I felt like I was home—not only in a physical way, but in my heart. Like my heart was home.

That's also why I couldn't resist hooking school and going to the zoo at Woodley Park. When I was old enough—about thirteen or fourteen—I'd hop the bus to Tenth Street and Pennsylvania Avenue, get on the subway, transfer at Metro Center, and then walk the ten blocks up to the zoo. It took about an hour to get there.

Almost as impressive to me as the raptors were the big animals—elephants, tigers, lions, hippos. They had power. You had to respect them. I began to understand at an early age that human relationships with anything wild require three things: love, patience, and most of all, respect. It sounds simple, but I would eventually learn that it's not easy at all. If something is untamed and wild, then it has a spirit that can't be crushed. That doesn't mean we should be afraid of it; it just means we have to take the time to learn about it and understand it. Once we understand the wild things, we understand ourselves. At least, that's what ended up happening with me.

I was still at the window, watching that hawk. It worked its prey back and forth in its beak until just the tail was hanging out, and then that was gone. We looked at each other, and the hawk let out a raspy scream that I could hear even through the closed window. I think it was proud to have an audience. He looked around for a moment, then spread its huge wings and took off with his red-orange tail feathers outspread. I pressed my face against the window so I could watch him glide in a rising current of air. I almost felt like I was flying away with him, beyond the rooftops, beyond the housing projects, beyond this drug deal, beyond the death and destruction.

"Hey, Rodney. What's out there? You want to finish this up or what?"

"Yeah, man. Yeah, yeah." I walked back over to the couch and took a close look at the scale. Looked like a perfect measurement of seven grams to me. I pulled a roll of hundred-dollar bills from my pocket and counted out $1,500, trying to avoid any pressure on my bandaged hand.

"Here you go, man," I said, handing T the money.

"Much obliged," T said with a laugh, carefully putting my dope into a glass vial. "See you in two weeks, Dog?"

"You know it," I said. I put the vial in my pocket, shook hands with T, and headed back into the heat.

⌣

At this time—the early 1990s—the city was still festering from the crack epidemic that had started in the late eighties. The lure of the drug crawled through and in and over the endless blocks of the DC housing projects like roaches in the cereal cupboard. Vacant-eyed addicts roamed the streets in search of the next hit. Even my mother was addicted to crack.

Young guys like me? Our lives could go in one of only three directions: professional athlete (c'mon, get real!), drug user (and lose all control over your life? No, thanks), or drug dealer (make good money, but either get shot and killed or go to jail). I chose Door Number Three.

I was never a street dealer. That was for people who wanted some quick cash rather than serious money. I didn't have time for the foolishness of street cred, turf wars, and stickup boys—they're the punks who rob the street dealers. I wanted to stay alive, and I wanted to make money. My business was on a higher level—I only bought good dope from serious dealers, and I only sold dope to serious dealers. In the hierarchy of drug dealers, I guess you could say I was mid-level.

But my housing was keeping me from growing my drug business, and I needed to do something about it quick. I was living in my mom's apartment at the Linda Pollin Memorial Housing projects. It was called "Linda Pollin" after real estate magnate Abe Pollin's daughter, who had died of a rare heart condition. A roomy public-housing development for working-class Black folks, opened in the late sixties—we called it the LP. People who had lived in the LP for a long time told me it had started going downhill in the 1980s, mostly because of tenant turnover, management problems, and endless maintenance issues. And then, like a thunderclap, came the crack cocaine epidemic. I dove right into the opportunity to make some good money. I remember laughing at a 1991 *Washington Post* article that called the LP the most lethal block in the city. The other dealers and I felt a weird pride about that tag. After all, what else did we have to be proud of?

But not having my own apartment was cramping my style. I needed more guns, but it would have been disrespectful of me to keep such an arsenal at my mom's place. My mom, Mary (aka Dippy), knew what I was doing, and she worried about me all the time—I could see it in her face—even when she was high. Whenever she talked about my drug dealing, her eyes grew dark. She worried about my older brother Chuck as well, especially when he drove up to New York to buy dope. He wasn't a street dealer, either. Mostly he just sold to the female strippers at the club where he bounced.

In addition to more guns, I needed to be able to make deals from my own place, on my own turf. The challenge was that most apartments wanted to see a few pay stubs to prove that a person could afford the rent. I could definitely afford it—I had thousands of dollars stashed away. But you don't get pay stubs or a W-2 from dealing drugs.

A buddy of mine had told me about a job fair happening at a community center of the nearby Valley Green housing project, and I decided to check it out. One table had a bunch of job listings and applications, and I found two that interested me. One was a maintenance position—my mom always gave me,

Chuck, and my sisters cleaning chores growing up, so I knew I could do that, at least for a couple of months so I could show some pay stubs. The other was a job with a group called Earth Conservation Corps (ECC), cleaning out the Anacostia River. That sounded good because, ever since I was a kid, if I had to choose between being outside or inside, it didn't matter how cold or hot it was, rain or shine, I wanted to be outside. Other kids might be inside watching TV, but I would rather be outside looking up at the sky. Something about rolling clouds, vast sky, and birds flying overhead spoke to me. But nature was like a foreign language. I wanted to understand the message it was trying to convey—I just couldn't make sense of the words.

The ECC people called me back first, so I accepted the position on the river. I was already familiar with the Anacostia. When I was little, our family would have cookouts at Anacostia Park. We'd swim in the river or just hang out with a bucket of KFC. Of course, we knew it was a general dumping ground for trash, but we didn't know how toxic the river really was.

Anyway, I went home and told my mom about the job. She was glad I was embarking on a legit job, even though she knew I would keep hustling. That was inevitable, as there was no way I could go from making several thousand dollars a week to a hundred. I was to start the new gig in a few days. I didn't know it then, but I was about to start learning the mysterious language of the birds and the sky and the ever-changing Anacostia River.

Chapter 2

Every once in a while, the Anacostia River still weaves its way into my dreams. Not in a big, bold, rushing-tumbling-splashing-symbolic kind of way. More like a quiet, in-the-background-but-always-there way. That's how it was this morning, right before I woke up. In the dream, I'm twenty-one again, in the river with Monique—she is still alive—and we are struggling to pull a dirty, water-logged mattress out of the river. We're both wearing hip-high waders and rubber gloves that the Earth Conservation Corps has given us.

"We need someone to help us, Rodney," says Monique, breathing heavily from the exertion.

"Naw, Monique, we got this. We're strong enough." It really is heavy, but no way am I going to admit that to Monique. I want to impress her with my strength, but this soaked mattress is brutal. I take a few backward steps up the riverbank, grab the top of the dripping mattress, and pull, while Monique stands in the water and pushes.

"Just. A. Little. Bit. More," I huff, accentuating each word with a yank on the mattress, as if that will give me some extra strength.

Finally the waterlogged mattress comes out of the river. As I take my final few steps, I slip in the mud and fall on my back, the mattress covering my legs.

"Monique, you pushed *too* hard!" I shout, but the scene is so ridiculous that I can't help but bust out laughing.

"Oh, you can take it," says Monique, climbing out of the water. "You just said we were strong enough." She flops on her back next to me in the swampy mud, and we both start laughing. In the dream, our laughter floats up to the cloudless summer sky, in the form of cartoon-like musical notes.

I wake with a start. I'm breathing heavily, and it takes me a second to realize where I am. These dreams always seem so real.

"Oh, Monique," I say to no one in particular, rubbing my eyes. "I wish you were still here."

I know that if I don't get up right away, the image of us finding Monique's lifeless body will come rushing back to me, and I can't have that chasing me all day when her murder already haunts me most nights. I throw back the blanket and walk into my compact bathroom. I brush my teeth, wash my face with soap and cool water, and stare at my reflection in the small mirror.

"No time for river memories today, old man," I say to my reflection. My sparse beard is flecked with gray—I'm forty-six, after all—but I'm totally content with whom I see in the mirror. I didn't always feel that way, though.

If anyone had told me twenty-five years ago that, at age forty-six, I would be a master falconer, caring for and training my own birds of prey, I would have laughed. Not so much about the falconry part—I've always loved animals—but mostly because I never expected to live that long, not with the life I was living.

I pull on the jeans and sweatshirt that are hanging over a chair and step into my worn, unlaced Timberland boots. It might be time to splurge on a new pair soon. "Got things to do," I say. I'm so used to talking to the birds, horses, and my dog all day that I end up talking to myself as well.

I step out of my trailer and shiver. It's only late September, but there's a bite of fall in the air. The sun is rising, but the chill has wrapped itself around the morning air. My horses, birds, and I live on property owned by the DC government near the Patuxent Wildlife Refuge.

Where I live has been designated as an animal sanctuary, and that's what it is. It's a sanctuary for me as well because, given the choice, I prefer to be around animals over people any day.

The Capital Guardian Youth Challenge Academy is also on the property. It's a five-and-a-half-month program—based on traditional military training—for young men and women who, I guess you could say, have lost their way or are very close to losing their way. They've dropped out of high school, they're getting into trouble, maybe hanging out with the wrong crew, or starting to try drugs. I see them as young people who crave change. They're desperate to either get out of their situation or reach for something better, but they feel like no matter what direction they go, it's the wrong one, and they don't know what to do. As part of their time with Capital Guardian, they have to do an internship with me, learning about wildlife, cleaning out cages, feeding the horses, and building aviaries. If they've used up any chances that they may have been given by anyone, as often as not Capital Guardian is their last hope to figure out how to build a life. That's kind of what Earth Conservation Corps helped me do, so I can relate to them. I also connect with them because I dropped out of high school during my junior year after getting in trouble with the police. When I see the kids from Capital Guardian, I see myself when I was that age—thinking I knew everything, but deep down inside wanting to see some kind of path for myself that wasn't covered with thorny brambles and weeds.

Here's the thing: when you grow up with limited means, in the inner city, with or without a stable family, and you're surrounded by the bounty that drug-dealing brings, and you're stuck in a shitty educational system that offers only a fraction of what rich kids get in their counties, you end up carrying all of the baggage that comes with that. And it's heavy—heavy like the wet mattress from my dream. Most crumple under the weight.

Working with the Capital Guardian kids means I get to do two of my favorite things: fly my raptors and show young people that they have options in their lives—they just have to keep an eye out for what ignites their heart, which sounds easier than it is.

On this particular day, like most others, I pull out my way-too-crowded key ring and fumble for the right key to the door of the storage building behind the trailer. This is where I keep feed for my four rescue horses, food for my raptors, and an assortment of carriers, extra gloves, jesses, and other falconry-related equipment. I grab a plastic bin out of the full-sized refrigerator, open it, and pull out a handful of dead white mice.

"Only the best, freshly thawed mice for my birds," I say out loud to no one.

As a licensed master falconer living close to Washington, DC, I'm able to purchase uncontaminated rats, mice, and small birds from the Envigo Laboratories at the National Institutes of Health. Because they've been bred at NIH, I know they are safe and not poisoned in any way. They arrive frozen, and I thaw them out for my raptors. Mice are what they eat in the wild, along with other rodents and rabbits. It's important that captive raptors be fed the same kind of diet they would eat if they were living in the wild. You can't just go to the grocery store and buy some raw meat—there's not enough nutrition in that for raptors.

I grab my leather glove that I need to handle the birds and the bunch of dead mice, and I'm ready to head across the lawn to the aviary. The mice bodies will stay fresh for a while because they aren't sitting out in eighty- or ninety-degree heat. I'll feed the raptors first and then the horses.

The five Harris's hawks I have now are Agnes, Nanny, Gloria, Chuck, and Squeal. Harris's hawks are social birds and even work together in the wild to get food. Agnes is my heart bird, given to me by a special person, Agnes Nixon, who was one of my staunchest supporters until her death last year. Sweet and docile Nanny and moody Gloria are named after two of my deceased aunts. Chuck is named after my older brother, and my soldier Squeal is named for by buddy Billy Morris.

I whistle to the birds as I make my way toward the aviaries.

"Time for breakfast, y'all," I call out.

Three aviaries are located in a semi-restored, 100-year-old barn. Two other aviaries are connected to the visitor's center, where I give presentations to various groups. I built all of the aviaries with help from friends and people from Earth Conservation Corps. This is a good spot for birds because one of the first things dedicated falconers must be sure they have is space. If a falconer is going to fly a red-tailed hawk, for example, then several acres of available fields are needed. I would discourage anyone from thinking about becoming a falconer unless they have located the right kind of space with natural prey like rabbits or small birds, depending on what your raptor hunts.

First up to get fed are Nanny and Gloria. I unlock the outside door, shut it behind me and then unlock the wood door to the first aviary. I created the double door entry to make sure the birds are safe from external disturbances. The United States Fish and Wildlife Service has general rules for aviary construction and maintenance, and officers from the Maryland Natural Resources Police come out regularly to check on my aviaries and the condition of my birds, to make sure I'm complying with all of the regulations.

Nanny and Gloria are in one of the larger aviaries,

sitting on perches across from one another. I imagine them gossiping and laughing with each other when I'm not around, just like my aunts used to do. With my gloved hand, I take one of the mice and hold it toward Nanny.

"C'mon, Nans."

She makes a little chirp and swoops across to land on my glove, grabbing the mouse with her curved beak. I shake my glove a little, and she flies back to her perch with her breakfast, the pink mouse tail hanging out of her mouth. I do the same thing with Gloria.

Falconry is a seasonal sport. In the spring my birds molt, dropping their old feathers and getting new growth. Falconers don't hunt their raptors in spring and summer because it's too easy to lose them in all of the foliage. During that time we feed them mice and keep them healthy. Around late August and September, I begin to feed them less and drop their weight to get them ready to hunt from about November through February. They have to be hungry when I fly them so that they return to me. That's why they don't get too much to eat today.

Falcons in captivity have a much higher chance for survival than those in the wild. It's safer for them to live in captivity because their chance of getting killed by cars or hunters is much lower, and the food they eat is safer.

At this point in my life, I know different raptors and their habits as well as I know the scars on my hands. I almost feel like I am one of them, although I'm not sure which one I'd be. Maybe I'm a Cooper's hawk, with its orange eyes and long, slender body. Or maybe a gyrfalcon, the largest and fastest of all falcons, with a regal white tail. Gyrfalcons mainly go for birds in flight, grabbing them in their beaks and breaking their necks so they die right away. Or maybe I'm just a regular old red-tailed hawk. Unlike falcons, most hawks are messy, mean killers. They sit in a tree and survey their surroundings, on the watch for a tasty morsel. Once a hawk spots an unsuspecting rabbit or squirrel, it swoops down, uses its sharp talons to pierce the skin, and then starts ripping into the furry skin with its beak, basically eating the prey alive. Nature at its fiercest.

That's the kind of stuff I think about when I'm working with my animals. The circle of life will always fascinate me more than any movie, book, or television show. Since I started working with birds, my motto has always been: Look Up. That's how you learn about birds and their habits. I've always taught my kids to look up. That's where you find the circle of life on full display. And if you're lucky, that's where you find hope.

I leave the girls and head over to the barn to feed the rest of the birds. Right inside the door is a wall with a bunch of writing on it: lots of names and poems. I think of it as a kind of prayer or memory wall, and I place my hand on it for a moment. I started it a few years ago after construction of the aviaries was completed. I wrote my mom's name—Dippy (that was her nickname)—and the names of other people I've known and loved who have passed. Over the years, I've invited every single person who comes to visit to write the name of a loved one they've lost on the wall. Doesn't matter who you are—everyone who comes here has lost someone they loved. This is a way to honor that person and keep their memory alive. It's a colorful, busy-looking wall, and it keeps energy and love flowing through the space. The aviaries are dedicated to those people who inspire us.

I finish feeding my hawks and an injured twenty-three-year-old Eurasian eagle-owl named Mr. Hoots, who belongs to Earth Conservation Corps but lives here for now.

As I walk toward the field and stable to feed the horses, the cell phone in my pocket starts to vibrate. It's my twenty-four-year-old son, Mike.

"Goober!" I yell into the phone. We've been calling him that practically forever because when he was little, we thought his head was shaped like a peanut. "What are you doing up this early?"

"Dad, I need to talk to you," Mike says.

"Well, go ahead and talk, then." I always like to get

to the point at hand, especially with my kids. No sense in wallowing around in chitchat.

"I want to become a falconer."

I stop walking toward the horses.

"Say that again."

"Dad. I want to be a falconer."

I let out a big scream of laughter, and I swear I can feel my chest swell a little. "Well, dang, it's about time you finally admitted it. When do you want to start?"

"Today."

"Well, all right then. I guess I'll see you later today."

I always knew that someday Mike would follow in my falconer footsteps—I just didn't know when. Even when he was little, I would see him watching birds with the same intent curiosity that I had.

"All right, Dad. I'll be over this afternoon." Mike pauses for a few seconds. "I want to be a falconer," he says again, ". . . like you."

I know Mike is proud of me, of the man I have become. I can hear it in his voice. But everything was different some fifteen years ago. Mike was only eight when I got locked up on drug charges. He later told me how he cried when one day I was just suddenly gone. He had seen other men in the neighborhood and his friends' fathers get locked up and never return. Mike thought that now it was *his* father's turn and that I might not be back.

Suddenly, it doesn't feel so chilly out here anymore. I head back to the storeroom to grab the feed for my four horses, Bailey, Dippy, Ninja, and Gnip. I let out a crazy whoop and start whistling for the horses. I'm glad Mike isn't here to see the goofy-ass grin I have on my face.

Chapter 3

1992

When your job is selling dope, you don't have to punch a time clock. That's why I didn't even own an alarm clock. My first day at the new nonprofit called Earth Conservation Corps—April 24, 1992—I had to show up at 8:00 a.m. I borrowed an alarm clock from a buddy and set it for 7:00.

ECC was only about ten minutes away, so I showered, put on some jeans and a T-shirt, and headed out. I stopped at the corner store to grab a doughnut and a Pepsi and walked toward the river.

In those days, the Anacostia River was like this mysterious, moving creature. Not only was it a dumping ground for all sorts of trash, but it was also known as a safe place to buy and sell drugs or to toss a dead body. More than once, someone would go missing and later their bloated body would be found, stuck among some old tires and plastic bottles in the Anacostia. Negative vibes from the river were almost as heavy as the humid, sticky air that hung over the stagnant water. One day this girl smoked a joint that was laced with PCP. She went wild, started screaming and shouting that she was burning up. She tore off her clothes and ran naked right into the Anacostia. As she was flailing and screaming, she got stuck amid debris and scummy water. She was rescued, but she was one of the lucky ones.

So that first day at ECC, I was already familiar with the landscape. Me, Anthony, James, Burrell, Monique, Tink, Benny, Deedee, and William—we were the first nine people hired. We were all in our late teens or early twenties and came from different housing projects in Southeast DC. Some of us knew one another or at least knew of one another. I knew Burrell because we had grown up together. But we all brought our "projects baggage" with us: attitude, street smarts, trash talk, suspicion of everything and everyone, and guns.

If you had a gun, you had it on you, and those of us who did didn't think twice about bringing one to the ECC job site. After all, we didn't know what we were getting into, so best to be prepared, just in case. I was twenty-one and at the height of my drug dealing, and I had fifteen guns at the time. My very first gun was a .25-caliber automatic nine-shot. It was easy to get firearms. Guns flowed back and forth through the projects just like the trash in the Anacostia River.

So there we were, a bunch of armed, know-it-all kids reporting for duty. The man who started ECC, Bob Nixon, put us to work, giving us waders and gloves. Even though it was only April, the morning was warm and sunny, and we all started to sweat as we struggled to pull up the heavy waders and learn how to walk in them. Of course we also had to hide our guns in backpacks or behind bushes before we got wet.

Into the water we went, pulling out tires, bikes, plastic bottles, and other debris. We were working in the Lower Beaverdam Creek, one of several tributaries of the Anacostia. The air was thick, not so much with the smell of trash but with the lack of oxygen. It was like this Anacostia creature was sucking up all of the good oxygen, and we were trying to clear its airways so it could breathe again. Looking up and down the water, I took in the mountains of trash and thought, *Man, ain't no way the nine of us are gonna make a dent in this. It'll take our whole lives.*

I didn't say that out loud, though. Didn't want to be accused of having a bad attitude on my first day of work.

We had all grown up near the Anacostia and knew it was filled with trash. What we didn't know was just how bad it was until we were actually in that filthy water, face to face with old bikes, tires, car engines, sofas, mattresses, sinks, bathtubs, car parts, and thousands of plastic bags and bottles. In just a few hours, our small, ragtag army had lugged piles and piles of crap into dumpsters. It was impressive, even to my skeptical eyes, and I thought, *Maybe we* can *do something here.*

In those early days of working in the Lower Beaverdam Creek, the area was what we called "the dead zone." On rainy or really humid days, a smell like rotten eggs would rise up from certain areas of the tributary. Except for a few little minnows and crawfish, no life was visible. We didn't even see any small birds, like robins or sparrows. It was as if a big sign was posted in the nature world that said "This Property Is Condemned," and all the wildlife took heed.

In the first three months, we hauled more than 5,000 car tires out of the river and ended up filling close to twenty huge dumpsters with river refuse. We called it The Dumping Ground River. At the end of each day I was exhausted, but I also felt like I had accomplished something important.

Learning about the Anacostia River was eye-opening for all of us. Native Americans lived on the Anacostia for about 10,000 years. For kids who were pretty much trying to stay alive just day-to-day, that amount of time was unimaginable. So what happened to the river? In a word—Europeans. European settlers came to the area in the 1600s and starting clearing most of the forests in the watershed to make room for tobacco plantations. Fast-forward to about 200 years later, and piles of toxic silt from the plantations had settled on the bottom of the river, making it impassable. No longer good for business, the river was basically abandoned. Into the twentieth century, no one could be bothered. And by that time, the only people living near the Anacostia were poor people like us, in the surrounding housing projects.

Over the weeks our tribe of nine started to bond with each other, working the ancient waterway. One day, several weeks in, a great blue heron landed nearby. We were all quiet for a moment. This was the first bird we had seen while working on the tributary, and it had landed on a spot that we had cleaned up. We started to cheer, and that scared the heron away, but we didn't care. We knew it would return because it had found a space free of trash. It was amazing how, after just a few weeks, we could see the bottom of the tributary and the water was beginning to flow.

For the first time in my life, I looked forward to getting up every morning and going to the river. That was a new sensation. Frankly, I really couldn't believe that I had survived to twenty-one. In the Southeast DC projects, staying alive into your twenties wasn't a reality for lots of us, so looking forward to something in the future, even just to the next day, was a luxury—and an unspoken rule was that you just didn't do that. Most of us had witnessed people—sometimes even friends and family—get shot and killed. So death was not just a number, a statistic, an item on the nightly news—this was straight-up reality for us, and I always knew I could be next.

My eight river co-workers became like a second family to me. I grew close to all of them, especially Monique. She wasn't that tall, but her personality was as big as the sky, and she was so funny. We were always cracking up at things Monique said or did. She had this loud, infectious laugh that made me smile. I called her my little sister even though she was two years older than me.

About four months into hauling trash out of the Anacostia, Bob Nixon—the ECC's founder and the guy who had hired us—saw the great job we were doing and how we had all become friends. One day he talked to us about taking a trip to Houston for about a month and a half or so to partner with another environmental group. We would be working with another group of young people to shore up a bayou that was washing away. We were definitely game. Some of us had never been to Texas. Hell, some of us had never even been out of Southeast DC.

Bob sent me and Anthony down several days ahead

of time to meet with the other group, assess the job, and organize a work schedule. We flew down there and rented a van at the airport. Houston in August didn't feel much different than DC in August—hot and muggy. Except the sun was a lot stronger in Texas. We rented an apartment in a small, modest complex, and Bob had subleased another apartment in the same complex from a guy who was traveling to California. That apartment was for Monique and Deedee.

Anthony and I spent those first few nights finding our way around Houston and checking out some of the clubs. The rest of the crew was supposed to come down later that week. On Tuesday, I got word that my uncle had died, so I had to fly back to DC.

Right before I returned to Houston on Friday, I learned that a friend of mine we called Lil Jesse had been shot and killed. On the plane back to Texas, I was stressed thinking about my uncle and Jesse. By the time the plane landed that night, my head was pounding with a migraine.

Anthony was in the driver's seat of the van we had rented, waiting to pick me up. Everyone else was in there too: Tink, Benny, William, James, and Monique. Burrell and Deedee had decided not to do the Houston job.

I headed toward the van, rubbing my forehead, when I heard shouting. My crew had jumped out and were cheering a welcome for me. I couldn't help but smile.

"You all are crazy, man!" I said.

They laughed.

"Come on, Rodney," said Anthony, grabbing my bag. "Get in the car. It's party time!"

I hugged everyone, and we piled into the car. "Naw, man," I said. "My head is splitting. I just want to go home and sleep."

"Uh-uh," said James. "We're doing it."

"C'mon, Rodney, please," begged Monique, grabbing my arm. "This is the first night we are all in Houston together. We have to celebrate. We have to."

I couldn't resist the pleas of my little sister.

"Aw, hell," I said. "Let's go."

We dropped my bag off at the apartment and headed to a club called Jamaica Jamaica, a reggae club that Anthony and I had checked out earlier that week.

The club was jumping, and my headache eased up once I had a drink. We spent the evening laughing and dancing to reggae music. Finally, around 1:30 in the morning, we'd had enough and drove back to the apartment complex.

Monique's apartment was in a building around the corner from ours, and we dropped her off there.

"G'nite, you all," she said.

"Bye, Shorty," I said. "We'll see you tomorrow."

Anthony and I got up early the next morning. Our

group and the one we were partnering with were being honored at a dinner that night for the environmental work we were doing. It was part of President George H. W. Bush's Thousand Points of Light Initiative. Bob, who was staying at a hotel, was going to pick up his father and a friend at the airport so they could attend the ceremony as well.

The others were still sleeping off the night of partying, so Anthony and I drove to the local mall to watch girls and hang out. We had to pick up some special shirts that we were all going to wear to the dinner that night.

By the time we finally got back to the apartment, it was about 2:00 in the afternoon. The guys were all there, but not Monique. It was getting late, and we had to start getting ready for the dinner.

"Tink, run over and tell Monique she has to get up and get over here," I said. "I have to make a phone call."

I wanted to call a buddy of mine back in DC to see how Lil Jesse's funeral had been.

Tink came back about ten minutes later, shut the apartment door behind him, and stared at us. I knew something was wrong and hung up the phone.

"Monique is dead," said Tink.

"That's not funny, man," I said. "Don't even be saying that shit."

"I'm telling you. Monique is dead. I saw her."

"You're wrong," I said, grabbing the keys to the van. We piled in and drove around the corner to Monique's building. Her apartment was on the lower level. I turned the handle; the door was unlocked.

"Monique," I called, knocking on the door as I was turning the doorknob. "Monique, you all right?"

"She ain't gonna answer," said Tink.

"Shut up, man," I said. And then I opened the door.

Only on television crime shows and in the movies had I ever seen so much blood. Straight ahead was a small kitchen with a breakfast bar. Blood on the walls, on the ceiling, on the floor, even on the kitchen stools. It was like if someone took a whole bunch of soda cans, shook them, opened them, and sprayed. Except this wasn't soda. Chairs and lamps had been turned over, pictures were on the floor. It was like a big barroom brawl had taken place.

In the middle of the living room floor was a huge puddle of blood. It looked like when you have a heavy trash bag that starts leaking and so you end up dragging it to the trash can, with all the stuff being dragged along. From the puddle, long smears of blood like skid marks on a street led down the hallway to the right toward where the bedroom and bathroom were. In my mind, there was no mistaking that someone had died. No way could anyone survive losing that much blood.

We followed the trail of blood down the hall and into the bedroom. From the bedroom you could see right into the bathroom, and there was Monique. She was naked in the bathtub, and her head, upper body, and arm were hanging over the side, lifeless. Her hand was just touching the floor, the same hand that mere hours ago had grabbed my arm, pleading with me to go to the club.

"Okay, we need to turn around and get the hell out of here and call the police," I said. We were all in shock.

The guys waited outside Monique's apartment while I drove back to ours and called 911. No cell phones in those days. Then I called Bob at his hotel, where he had just arrived from the airport with his friend and his father.

I ran back to Monique's apartment, and we waited in silence for the police. None of us were strangers to death and murder, but the extreme violent nature of what we saw there shook us to our cores.

The sirens started far away and got louder. Two police cars pulled into the parking lot and cops jumped out, guns drawn.

"Get on the ground," they shouted. "Get on the ground."

All six of us knew the drill, and we got on the ground.

"Look, man," I said. "I'm the one who called you all. We're her friends, and we're the ones who found her."

"Yeah, she's gone," one of them said. "Looks like she was shot three times."

Anthony and I looked at each other. Shot? How could someone be shot three times in a basement apartment and none of the neighbors heard anything?

By this time Bob, his father, and his friend pulled up. Bob was explaining to the cops who Monique was and then more officers and a medical examiner arrived. We went back to our apartment because the cops said they wanted to question us. They said they thought Monique had been shot seven times and stabbed. We learned later that she hadn't been shot at all. What the cops at first thought were bullet holes were punctures from the claw end of a hammer where the killer had beat her to death.

Things were getting tense in the apartment. The cops said that Monique had fought her attacker, and that there was skin and blood under her nails. They wanted to check us for scratches. We were starting to get pissed. Bob pulled me into one of the bedrooms.

"Look, Rodney," he said. "If you don't agree to letting them check you for scratches, then the others won't either, and this whole thing is going to get even worse."

We left the bedroom. "Okay, everyone," I said to the crew. "Let's take our shirts off." It was humiliating for the five of us to be standing there shirtless, while the cops examined our bodies. But we also would do any-thing to help find Monique's killer.

Tink had four scratches on his shoulder, and he explained that they were from his cat. We could all see that the scratches weren't fresh, but that was all it took. The cops decided to zero in on Tink.

We all ended up being taken to the police station so they could question us individually. By the time we left, it was after ten at night. We were emotionally stunned and physically exhausted. Bob put us up at a nice, quiet hotel called the Allen Park Inn. That day—August 17—was the longest day of my life.

The next morning, Bob's father took us horseback riding for a couple of hours to try and get our minds off the horror we had seen. But I couldn't stop thinking about how we might have prevented Monique's death. If only we had taken her back to our apartment to hang out instead of dropping her off. If only we hadn't gone to the club at all, maybe we could have somehow kept it from happening.

The police came to the hotel later that day. They wanted Tink's clothing and took his fingerprints. The next day—Monday—we learned that the prints didn't match. Tink was cleared.

On Tuesday, we all flew back to DC, and it wasn't soon enough. I wasn't sure any of us would really recover from this.

A few days later, we went to Monique's funeral. People had heard about Tink being questioned, and rumors were flying that he had done it, even though the police had cleared his name. I took two of my guns to the funeral because if anyone tried to do anything to Tink in a misplaced sense of revenge, then they were going down.

The funeral happened without incident, though, and then it was over, but we were changed forever.

About a week later, the man from whom we had sublet the apartment was arrested and charged with Monique's murder. According to the police, George Wayne Demery let himself into the apartment and tried to rape Monique. She fought back and so he beat her to death.

In 1995 we returned to Houston to testify at Demery's trial, where we learned that after beating her, he cut her wrists and dragged her to the bathtub to make it look like a suicide. I stared at Demery in the courtroom. He looked like a gargoyle to me, and I hated him. He was sentenced to death but ended up dying in prison several years later.

I was suicidal after Monique's death. I just didn't see any reason in living. What was the damn point? I couldn't wrap my head around the kind of evil that would do something so vicious to Monique. I couldn't sleep, and neither could Bob or Anthony. We'd call one another in the middle of the night.

"You up?"

"Yeah, man, can't sleep. Keep seeing it all in my head."

"Me too, man, me too."

I used to have to keep the bathroom door in my apartment shut all the time, because anytime I would look in there, I would see Monique in the tub. You could see the bathroom from my bedroom, so I took to sleeping on the living room couch.

Our group, our river family, was fractured. Monique's death had shattered our enthusiasm, our resolve, and our spirit. Once we returned to DC, the eight of us talked.

"That's it for me and ECC," I said. "I'm done." I wasn't going to stay and wait around for the next one of us to die.

"C'mon, man," said Burrell. "If we stop right now, then no one will know about Monique. It's up to us to keep her memory alive."

We all talked back and forth for a long time and, in the end, we agreed that the best way to honor Monique was to continue the work that she had been a part of. We decided to stay. And we didn't know it then, of course, but Tink would be the next in our group to be murdered.

I knew that going back to work on the Anacostia wouldn't make the pain stop. But neither would not going. Nothing stops that kind of pain once it's ripped through you.

Little by little, we all got back to the work of cleaning up the river. I also returned to my flourishing drug-dealing business, but the Anacostia River kept drawing me back.

About two years after Monique was killed, Bob Nixon told us he wanted to see if we could work on bringing bald eagles back to DC. He said the birds of prey hadn't been in the area in decades.

My reaction? Oh hell, yeah. I had always been fascinated with birds, especially the big ones like hawks, owls, falcons, and vultures. And there was that weird interaction I'd had with the hawk when I was making that drug deal. Somehow all of this felt connected, but I didn't know exactly how.

And now, here was the chance to actually raise and maybe even touch a bald eagle? Once again, I told Bob Nixon to count me in.

On my way back to my apartment, I decided to stop by my mom's to tell her about the eagles. She had started getting really into the work I was doing on the Anacostia, and she cried with me after Monique died.

It was a typical humid summer day in DC. Sun burning down on the cement, and air heavy with moisture. It was the kind of afternoon that would likely end in a thunderstorm when the baking temperatures and heavy humidity would start churning together and create unstable air that would rise until . . . *BOOM!*

I cut through the narrow, maze-like sidewalks between the buildings of the Linda Pollin housing project, where my mother lived. When I got to her building, I ran down the seven steps to her apartment on the lower level.

I knocked and pulled my key ring out of my jeans pocket.

"Hey, Ma, it's me," I called, picking out the right key. I opened the door onto a little hall that led into the living room. Beyond that was the dining room, and the kitchen was around the corner.

The curtains were drawn to help keep the apartment cool. Mom wasn't in the living room. I heard some faint music coming from the radio she kept in the kitchen. Ma liked to listen to the '70s soul music station while she washed dishes.

"Mom," I called again, heading back to the kitchen.

There she was, sitting at the same wooden kitchen table we'd had since we kids were little. She looked up at me but didn't say a word.

In front of her on the table was all of the drug paraphernalia she had accumulated over the years: small glass pipes; lighters; old spoons, black from being used to cook crack; pieces of tin foil; steel wool; rolling papers; and short pieces of straws. It was all spread out on the kitchen table, and she was just staring at it.

"Ma, what's going on? What are you doing? Are you okay?"

She finally looked up at me, as though she was just registering my presence. She took off her glasses and rubbed her hand over her eyes. Then she looked at me again.

"Rodney," she said, pausing for a moment, "I'm done. I. Am. Done. With all of this." She waved her hand over the table. "I don't want to do any of it anymore. Not weed, not coke, and especially not crack."

She put her glasses back on, propped her chin on her hand and looked at me again as if to say, "So what do you think about that?"

A boom of thunder pierced the air, and rain began to pound against the kitchen window.

Mom had never been a hardcore addict, but she had always used, probably more recreationally than anything, because she had no problem raising us four kids by herself and holding down a job, but the drugs were always there. Until today, that is. I sat down at the table with her, and we talked about her decision. I knew it would stick, because the one thing you could say about Mary Stotts—or Big Dippy, as her brothers and sisters called her—was that once she decided to do something, she was all in—100 percent. When we kids were little, we used to laugh and say, "When Dippy talks, people listen, just like E. F. Hutton," referring to a popular television commercial at the time.

After I told her about the eagles, as I was getting ready to walk out the door that day and return to my own apartment, Mom stopped me.

"You know, Rodney, now that my mind is going to be crystal clear 24/7, I'm gonna be worrying about you even more than I do now, and you know that's a lot. And your brother Chuck, too. I don't want you all to get killed. I don't know what I would do."

My mom had this way of looking at me when she was worried, and her eyes just pierced my soul. She was afraid I would end up in prison or worse—dead.

I kissed her cheek. "I know, Ma. I won't. You know I'm always careful, always watching my back. Same with Chuck."

I left and tried to push the guilt out of my mind. I hated making my mom worry, but I had to make a living.

Chapter 4

2017

I have thoughts about why Mike has finally decided that now is the time to become a falconer, but I need to hear it from him. It's about three in the afternoon, and Mike is due to arrive any time now for his first falconry lesson. I'm rooting around in the storeroom, gathering some equipment and my copy of the *California Hawking Club Apprentice Manual*, which I've found to be the best guide for a new falconer. It covers much of the material in the test that Mike will need to take in order to reach the apprentice level.

Becoming an "apprentice," the first level of falconry, requires someone to work with a master falconer—who is also their sponsor—for two years. But before someone can even reach the apprentice level, they have to take a test with about fifty-five questions and get at least 80 percent of them correct. The test is administered by a state's department of fish and wildlife. Once someone passes the test, they are an official apprentice falconer. The next level is general falconer, and this calls for experience with raptors and hunting with your bird. The final level to attain is master falconer—that's what I am—and requires at least eight years' experience. Falconry is a time-consuming sport that requires dedication and focus, and Mike has plenty of both. But he's only at the beginning of the process, and he has a lot to learn.

A car crunches onto my gravel and dirt driveway, and I hear Mike's sign of arrival: two short beeps on the car horn, a pause, and three more beeps.

"Hello, hello," I call as Mike climbs out of the car. I toss him the manual, and we hug. "So why now?" I ask.

"Aw, c'mon, Dad," he says. "You know why."

About three months ago, Mike and I had what I can only call a spiritual experience. Let me put it this way: when it was all over, I broke down crying, and I'm not exactly the crying type.

"Dad, when I saw you at the top of that fence, some thirty, forty feet high, trying to grab that bald eagle, I thought, *Man, this dude is trippin'*," Mike says, laughing at the memory.

"It was quite a day," I say.

In addition to being a DC fireman, Mike also picks

up the occasional side hustle. Lately, in his off hours, he's been working as a guard at a federal Homeland Security building, not far from the Anacostia metro station.

On the day he's referring to, I was on Valley Avenue in Southeast DC, hanging with my man Cornelius—everybody calls him Unk because he's like an uncle to the neighborhood. It was June 28—the second anniversary of my mom's death. Unk and I go way back—to when we were young men thinking we were invincible.

We were probably in our late teens when we met. Unk and I had seen each other on the streets and at pickup games on the basketball courts. We were both good players—some of the guys called us beasts on the courts—because we could beat anyone who dared to play us. It was all about the layup, the jump shot, and the dunk. Some crazy player would always come along, thinking they could beat us, but Unk and I were fast, and we were tall. Now, don't get me wrong—we weren't the Harlem Globetrotters, but we'd fancy-foot around any dude who thought he could take us on, and then we'd just dunk on him. Then he'd be all embarrassed because we'd run circles around him, and the fool would want to try again. And he'd get embarrassed again. It was hilarious.

Unk and I started hanging at each other's houses, and soon became as close as blood brothers. We even started calling each other's mothers "Mom." One day, years after we first met, we were sitting on Unk's porch talking and he was telling me a story about something crazy he had done. He said, "Man, Wilma was pissed off at me." I said, "Wilma? Who the hell is Wilma?" Unk started laughing. "That's my mom, man!" We'd been calling each other's mothers "Mom" for so long, we had no idea what their first names were.

My mom loved Unk as much as she loved any of her children. If she was driving down the street and saw Unk on the corner, she would always holler and wave and stop to make sure he wasn't getting into any trouble, which he probably was.

So anyway, on that day about three months ago, Unk and I were sitting outside on his porch, sharing stories about my mom and the old days. Even though two years had passed since she died, I still missed her like crazy. She was such a force in our lives, and she had overcome so much. When my mom was about six months pregnant with me, my father beat her, and I ended up being born prematurely at Fairfax Hospital. As soon as I was released from the neonatal intensive care unit, my mom left my father and took me and my older brother and sister—Chuck and Shanell—and moved into Valley Green housing projects with her mother and father. Mom was tough, fearless, and determined to raise us on her own. It sounds ridiculous, I know, but I figured she could overcome death just like she had all the other hardships in her life.

Mom had heart issues for several years, and she had a pacemaker that needed to be adjusted. It sounded like a pretty ordinary procedure, and it was scheduled for a Monday at Washington Hospital Center. That night, after the surgery, my sister called and put Mom on the phone.

"Hey, Dippy," I said. "How did it go?"

"I love you, Rodney," my mom said. Her voice sounded weak and strained, not like her usual bright and full tone.

"I love you. I love you," she said again, practically whispering.

"Well, I love you too, Fat Girl," I said, trying to sound cheerful, but I didn't know why she kept saying that.

The next morning, I learned something hadn't gone right with the surgery, and Mom needed another procedure. Dang. That didn't sound good. I was driving to the hospital after the second surgery when my son, Mike, called me.

"Goober," I answered.

"Dad, Grandmom's gone," he said, crying. "She's in a coma."

"What are you talking about? I just talked to her last night," I said.

"Dad, I'm here at the hospital. She had the second surgery, but she's not waking up. I don't think she's gonna make it, Dad. You have to come quick. She's on a machine, and we have to decide what to do."

It all seemed so unreal. I pulled my van into the hospital parking lot and ran down the hallway to my mom's room. Chuck and my sisters were already there with Mike, and some other family members soon arrived. We all crowded into the small room and stood around Big Dippy's bed, our hands on her legs and arms, trying to channel healing into her damaged heart.

The doctors said she had slipped into a coma after the second surgery, and they couldn't detect any brain activity. A machine was keeping her alive, and we knew we'd have to make a decision.

My mom always insisted that she never wanted to be hooked up to a machine. She used to say, "When the Father calls me, do *not* interrupt that call."

It was June 24, and Chuck suggested that we let Mom stay on the machine for a few days so family and friends could say their goodbyes.

We took turns holding Dippy's hand. Whenever one of us would say something like "Mary, do you want to stay on this machine?," her heart monitor would make a little blip. We believed that meant she was getting "the call," and we knew what we had to do.

Four days later—June 28—the doctors unplugged Mom from the machine at 11:00 a.m. She looked like she was sleeping. About two hours later I told her, "Look Ma, I got to run home and feed the animals and birds. I won't be gone long. Now listen to me, you have to wait until I get back. You cannot leave before I get back, you understand? I will be back soon."

I jumped into the van and sped out of the parking lot. Once home, I fed the birds, the horses, and my dog, threw on a clean T-shirt, and hightailed it back to the hospital. I got back to the hospital at 3:30. My brother and sisters were there. I rubbed Ma's arm. "I'm back, Dip," I said. "Just like I said I would."

My brother Chuck didn't say a word, but big, fat tears were rolling down his cheeks and dropping onto Ma's bed. At exactly 4:02 p.m., Mom opened her eyes wide, looked at us for just a second, and then closed them. She was gone.

That was two years ago, although sometimes it seems like it was yesterday. That's why, sitting on Unk's porch a few months ago, we both had tears in our eyes, remembering my mom's death. We started talking about Mom's homegoing service when my phone rang. It was Mike.

"Hey Goober, what's up?" I answered.

"Dad, Dad, there's a bald eagle stuck in a fence," said

Mike. He was agitated and shouting. Mike was at his side job as a guard at a Homeland Security base off of Highway 295 in an area thick with trees.

"A bald eagle?" I said, thinking, *No way, that's impossible.* "You sure?"

"Yes, I'm sure. It's stuck in a fence at Homeland Security, and it's setting off the alarm system. I think it's hurt."

"I'll be right there." I jumped up and dug in my pocket for the car keys.

"Catch you later, Unk," I called, running toward the van. "Goob's found an eagle stuck in a fence."

Valley Avenue is only a couple miles from the Homeland Security site, and I made it there in about ten minutes. I grabbed a leather glove from the back of the van and ran to the fence where Mike was standing. Several other guards were shaking the fence, trying to free the eagle, which only made the frantic bird wedge itself even more tightly into the fence.

Mike saw me pull up and waved the other guards to leave. "My dad's here," I heard him say. "We'll take it from here." They started walking back to their posts, only too happy to let this be someone else's problem.

From the ground, I could see that it was indeed a bald eagle. Judging by its dark head and tail and brown and white feathers, I guessed it to be a juvenile female, probably between one and two years old. Juvenile eagles go through several phases of coloring until they reach adulthood at about four years of age, when their heads are white, their beaks a golden yellow, and their feathers dark. This girl was stuck in the top of the fence, about thirty feet up. Her neck was wedged between two tight forks in the fence, and she looked frightened and exhausted. But she was alive.

"How long has she been here?" I looked at Mike.

"I'm not sure," he said. "I just came on duty."

"Okay, well, let's go," I said.

I tightened my grip on my bird glove and started to climb the fence. I had to shimmy up, mainly using my hands and arms because my boots were too big to fit between the chain links of the fence. I also had to make sure I didn't drop the glove. I turned my feet out and tried to use the grooves on the bottom of my boots to cling to the fence. I must have looked like some kind of scrawny duck.

"God, Dad, be careful," Mike shouted from below.

"I'm good, I'm good," I called back, even though I wasn't at all sure about that.

My right foot slipped, and my leg dangled for a second until I was able to get a grip again. My arms were starting to ache from doing all the work, but I couldn't stop now. And I was afraid that if I paused even for a second, I would get disoriented and fall, likely breaking a few bones in the process. Finally, I reached the top, out of breath, with some scrapes and scratches on my arms. I was about two feet away from the eagle, and she was in distress: breathing heavy, trembling, but not making a sound. Fear had stolen her voice. Some years ago, a friend of mine had been jumped at gunpoint. I asked her why she hadn't screamed, and she said it was as if her fear was a hand that grabbed her throat, and she couldn't make a sound, like in those dreams where you try to scream but nothing comes out. I was worried that the terrified eagle might go into shock or have a heart attack.

"All right, girlie-girl," I whispered to the eagle. "You're gonna be fine. Just give me a second, okay? You'll be free soon. I promise."

I hung onto the fence with my left arm and hand and put the glove in my mouth to free my right hand. I took off my belt and managed to loop it through the fence wire, essentially tying myself to the fence so I wouldn't fall to my death.

"Dad, what are you doing? Is that belt gonna hold you?" Mike shouted.

"It keeps my pants up, right? Now it just has to hold me up," I said, trying to make a joke.

I wiggled my right hand into the glove and gently reached over to the eagle, talking softly to her the whole time. I grabbed her shaking body and used my forefinger to gently dislodge her head from the fence prongs.

My plan was to climb down the fence with the bird and then check her for injuries, but I soon realized that would be a stupid and dangerous thing to do. There was no way I could climb down that fence using just one hand. What would be gained if we fell to the ground? Then we'd both be hurt . . . that's if we survived. Time for Plan B.

"Dad, you got her out," Mike shouted.

"Yeah, I know, but I can't make it back down with her. I'm gonna have to turn her around and let her go," I called down to Mike. My mouth was dry, and my heart was beating like conga drums. "Just give me a second." I would have to hold the eagle kind of sideways, but if her talons or wings were damaged, she would fall to the cement thirty feet below and surely die. In that moment, as I was assessing my very limited options, I realized that I had to be the landing gear for this eagle and it was critical that I position her properly to fly, if she could. I was not happy about releasing her under these treacherous terms, but I had no choice.

I looked into the eagle's brown eyes; they lighten up to yellow once they become adults. "You have to try real hard to fly now," I said. And then it hit me—dang! This was one of two young bald eagles that had been born about a year earlier in a nest about a quarter of a mile away. The eaglets were the offspring of two adult eagles released several years ago by Earth Conservation Corps. We had installed a camera nearby to watch the eaglets hatch and grow. In fact, I named the female baby—the one I now had in my hand—Dippy—after my mom, because she was hatched around the time Ma died. That really blew my mind, but I couldn't think about that now; I had to save this eagle.

"Ok, Mike. On three."

"One," Mike shouted from below.

"Okay, Dippy girl," I said softly to the eagle. "You got this."

"Two," called Mike. "Three."

I turned my wrist over so Dippy was right side up, moved my arm up in the air, and let go. She flew. Dippy flew.

Mike and I cheered at the same time. My glove fell to the ground. The young eagle landed in a nearby tree and started making quick, high-pitched chirps. *Ki-ki-ki-ki-ki-ki.* I believed Dippy was thanking me.

I unfastened my belt from the fence and slowly made my way back down the fence. When my feet hit the ground the emotion of the situation hit me, and I started to cry. I hugged Mike, even though I was sobbing.

"Dad, what's wrong?" said Mike. "You saved it."

"That was Dippy," I said, wiping my tears with the back of my scratched hand. "That's my ma."

"Grandma? What are you talking about, Dad?"

After wiping my face with my sweat-covered T-shirt, I explained to Mike how I had named the young juvenile female Dippy, after his grandmother. It had to be her. It wasn't like those woods were crawling with juvenile female bald eagles.

On that day—the second anniversary of my mom's death—a young eagle named Dippy found her way to me.

"Mike, that was Mom telling me she's all right," I said, tearing up again.

Mike started crying too, and we hugged again, as Dippy the eagle still chattered from the treetop.

"And that's when I knew it was time for me to become a falconer," Mike says, looking through the apprentice manual and bringing us both back to the present. "Dad, you had fire and determination in your eyes that day. You were willing to get hurt to save that eagle, to do something you really believe in. I was so amazed and proud of you that day. And now, here I am."

I laugh. "Yeah, you're never gonna be able to top what I did that day," I say. Mike and I have always had a friendly competition with one another in just about everything.

Mike laughs, too. "Yeah, and the sad thing is, I was the one who gave that to you. Don't worry, though— I'll top that rescue one of these days. Just wait."

"Ha ha. I won't hold my breath, though," I say, grabbing Mike by the shoulder. "And right now, it's time for you to have your first falconry lesson. Let's go."

Chapter 5

1993

I wanted to kill Anthony. It's true that just about an hour earlier he had pulled me out of the Anacostia after I got stuck in some mud and trash. But I still wanted to do some serious physical damage to him, and I had the will and the weapons to do it. I was so sick of his bullshit, and I wanted to shut him up once and for all. Our group of nine at Earth Conservation Corps—well, now eight since Monique was murdered—got along pretty well for the most part, except for me and Anthony. It was never lukewarm with the two of us. We were either tight, talking about girls, laughing it up, or we hated each other. Like earlier that morning, I was minding my own business, pulling trash out of the Anacostia River and tossing it up on the bank to go into the dumpster. A few yards away I saw the top of a tire sticking out of the water. As I waded over to get it, my feet were suddenly sucked into the mud and muck, and water started flowing into my waders, weighing me down even more.

"Yo, I need some help here," I shouted to the others. Anthony was the closest, and he ran along the riverbank and then waded in.

"Grab my hand, Rodney," he said.

I had to really stretch because I couldn't move my feet out of the mud. He came in a step closer and grabbed my hand.

"You gotta pull your feet out," he said.

"Don't you think I know what I 'gotta' do?" I said, irritated that I needed Anthony's help.

He pulled, and I was able to yank my feet out and make it back to the shore. We were both out of breath.

"You're welcome," said Anthony.

"Yeah, yeah," I said, and went to my backpack to find some dry jeans.

Some days it was like Anthony just had to say something that he knew would get under my skin, and then I would have to give it back to him. If I said something was black, he swore it was white. He would just poke and poke. C'mon, man, quit that shit. And he would always end the trash talk by bragging about his Glock, which he kept in his backpack when he came to ECC.

As the day wore on, for reasons that I still don't

know, the words became different, rougher, raw. Maybe because it was summer, and the stifling heat and humidity was getting to everyone, I don't know. But the tension between the two of us was high, and I just wanted him to go away. I could feel my anger inching toward the point of no control, like when you see lightning and you know a big thunder boom is about to happen.

Anthony started talking about how everyone was afraid of him because he was tough and because they knew he had a powerful gun.

"Man, I'm so tired of you talking about your goddamned Glock," I said, stepping a little closer to him.

"What are you gonna do?" Anthony said, standing his ground. "You can't whoop me, Slim. I'm bigger, and I'm for sure badder."

At around 240 pounds, Anthony definitely outweighed me. I was 150 pounds. But what did I need weight for? I had ammunition.

"That Glock is shit," I said. "But go ahead; you keep talking. Today is Friday. I promise you, Anthony, you ain't gonna be here on Monday. You are not going to be here."

Anthony lived in the Valley Green housing project, and I had lots of family and friends around that way. Once I put the word out, I would have no problem tracking down Anthony over the weekend and teaching him a lesson. No way could that old Glock protect him from the weapons I had, plus I was pretty sure I was a much better shot than he was.

Bob Nixon got wind of the threats we were lobbing to each other, and came over to separate us. He took me aside and asked what was going on.

"Bob, I swear to God, I am not backing down from that fool, and I got the guns that say I don't have to." I had so much anger inside, and I wasn't even sure that it was all directed toward Anthony, but I didn't know what else to do with it. I had the notion that shooting Anthony would relieve my anger.

"He thinks his Glock is all that. Well, let me tell you, some of my guns have clips that are bigger than his Glock." I was agitated and gesturing with my arms.

Bob looked at me for a few seconds, and then said, "C'mon, you're going with me."

"Where?"

"We're spending the weekend at my mother's house in Pennsylvania," said Bob, herding me toward his car. "I think it would be good for you to be away from this situation for a little while. We'll stop at your apartment so you can get some clothes."

I didn't know whether to go with Bob or to tell him to go to hell. My urge to punish Anthony was strong. In the end, I wound up going with Bob. If he could get me out of the stinking projects for a weekend, maybe that was a good thing.

Bob drove me to my apartment at 3838 South Capitol Street. We climbed the stairs to the third floor, and I unlocked the multiple deadbolts on the door. When Bob walked in, he stopped and let out a small whistle. I followed his gaze to the middle of the living room, where a large cardboard box sat on the floor. The box had held my 50-inch television, but now it was home for my guns: some handguns as well as the big boys: the AK 47, the SKS, the Chopper, the 44 Desert Eagle, they were all sticking out of the box.

Bob looked at the box, looked at me, and said, "You gotta be kidding me, Rodney."

"What, man, you thought I was lying about my weapons?"

Bob walked over, peered in the box and looked at me. "Just go pack your clothes," he said.

I threw some clean jeans, underwear, and T-shirts into my backpack along with my toothbrush and a washcloth and walked back into the living room.

"I'm just about ready," I said, rummaging through the box of guns. Since I was going to someone's house, I thought a small handgun would be the best choice.

"What are you doing?" Bob asked.

"I'm deciding what gun to bring."

"God, Rodney. You can't bring a gun to my mother's house."

"But I never go anywhere without a gun," I replied.

"Trust me, you won't need a gun."

I shrugged. A gun-free weekend would be a whole new experience for me.

We climbed into Bob's Volkswagen and got onto Interstate 295, headed toward Interstate 95. I knew this route like the back of my hand. Even though I was working for Bob at ECC, I was still dealing drugs, and my brother Chuck and I would often head up 95 to New York to buy drugs. This time though, Bob and I drove through Baltimore and stopped at the Maryland House rest stop for snacks. Bob called his mom to tell her when we would arrive and said he was bringing me along.

During the drive, Bob told me about his mother, Agnes Nixon. I didn't know her from a can of paint, but Bob said she was a big deal in the world of soap operas. She was the creator of *One Life to Live*, *All My Children*, and *Loving*. I knew something about those soaps—they were the ones my mom watched when she wasn't working at the Silver Hill Dry Cleaners. On those days, the television would be on from 12:30 to 3:00 so my mom could watch her stories. According to Bob, his mother had won a bunch of writing awards, including some Emmys. He confessed that he had shared my journal with her. During the first months of working at ECC, Bob had encouraged all of us to keep journals about our lives and how we felt about working on the Anacostia. I didn't care if Bob showed mine to his mom. Even though I had never been star-struck, I looked forward to meeting Miss Nixon because she sounded interesting and because she had created the stories that my mom watched.

Bob Nixon also had a pretty interesting story. He was a Hollywood movie producer, and his home base was in California. The only reason he wound up in the bowels of Southeast DC was because of the environmentalist Dian Fossey, who worked with gorillas in Rwanda. Bob had met her when he was shooting a film in Africa, and he wanted to produce a movie about her life. Fossey was murdered in 1985, but before that happened, she agreed that Bob—who also had strong interest in wildlife and the environment—could tell her story on one condition: he had to commit to at least one year of hands-on work on a conservation project. It wasn't until after Fossey's death that Bob co-produced the hit movie *Gorillas in the Mist*. After all the chatter about the movie died down, Bob started to think about how he would keep his word to Dian Fossey. One day he read an article in the *New York Times* about the polluted Anacostia River in DC and he said it was like a light bulb went off. He wanted that to be the project he would take on to honor Fossey's request. Not only did he want to help clean up the Anacostia, but Bob wanted to recruit the kids from the neighboring housing projects to help. Not just any kids, though. Bob wanted to recruit the kids who were getting in trouble, the dropouts, the drug dealers, the violent ones—the kids nobody wanted to help. And so Earth Conservation Corps was born. Sometimes I laugh to myself thinking Bob had no idea what he was getting into with our band of tough, streetwise kids, and now here he was driving one of them—me—out of state to keep me from killing someone.

It was early evening when we arrived in Philadelphia. Bob wanted to stop at a bookstore where a writer friend of his was giving a reading. We stayed at the bookstore for a couple of hours and then drove to Bob's mom's house about thirty minutes away in a neighborhood called Rosemont.

As we got closer, I could tell this wasn't your average white-bread suburb. This was rich people's world. Like, really rich people. Bob drove slowly through the tree-lined streets past mansion after mansion—brick ones, stone ones, some with pools. He slowed down and turned the car into the driveway of what he described as an "eighteenth-century colonial house." I just called it *fancy*.

"Well, I'm sure they didn't have these tennis courts and pool in the seventeen hundreds," I said.

"Well, my parents made a few minor improvements to the house." We both cracked up.

As we made our way down the driveway to the sprawling house, we passed lush fruit trees and neatly clipped shrubs. I wasn't in Southeast DC anymore—that was for sure.

It was after ten o'clock as Bob unlocked the front door. I wasn't sure Miss Nixon would still be awake.

"Mom, we're here," Bob called, and I followed him down a hall to a big, bright country kitchen. In front of the stove stood one of the most petite women I had ever seen. She had shoulder-length blond hair and bold blue eyes and was wearing a velour-type tracksuit. She put her hands on her hips and cocked her head to one side.

"Mom, this is Rodney Stotts. Rodney, this is my mom, Agnes Nixon," said Bob.

"Nice to meet you, Miss Nixon," I said.

She paused for a second and then said, "Hello, Rodney. I hope you left your arsenal in the car."

She and I busted out laughing, and Bob just rolled his eyes. I appreciate a good sense of humor, and this woman seemed to get me on some level.

"Yes, ma'am," I said, still laughing. Turns out Bob had told her about the situation with me and Anthony.

Miss Nixon told me to make myself at home and said that Bob and I could help ourselves if we wanted something to eat or drink. Then she said that she was going to bed and would talk to us in the morning.

Bob handed me a soda and showed me to my room on the second floor, which was of course bigger and fancier than any bedroom I'd ever slept in at the projects.

The next morning, I woke up, went into the bathroom that was attached to my bedroom, and took a shower. The comfortable smell of fresh coffee filled the house, and I went downstairs to the kitchen. The coffee maker was on the counter along with several mugs. I spied a yellow bowl of sugar on the table, and I heaped several spoonsful into my cup of steaming joe. Gotta have that sugar.

"Rodney, is that you?" came a voice from the bottom of the basement stairs.

"Yes, is that you, Miss Nixon?"

"Yes. Come down and talk to me."

I carried my coffee downstairs. Miss Nixon was dressed in a white T-shirt and sweatpants, and she was walking on a treadmill. I guessed that was why she was so trim.

"Good morning," she said. "I can make you some eggs or something if you'd like."

"No thanks. I found the coffee, and that's all I need for now."

"Good," she said, still walking. "Sit down and talk to me while I finish my miles."

As petite as she was, I got the sense that Agnes Nixon wasn't someone to be messed with, so I sat down.

"I read your journal," she said. "You're a good writer. Have you thought about writing a book?"

I laughed. Writing a book? I thought maybe I was wrong about this lady understanding me. My life was about drugs, guns, running the streets, staying alive, and—more and more lately, I had to admit—Earth Conservation Corps.

"Miss Nixon, I'm not a writer. You're the writer. Is it true you've even won some Emmy awards?"

She smiled. "It's true, but what's really been important over the years is doing what makes me happy. I knew early on in life that I would only be happy if I followed my heart."

I thought about that. How could I possibly follow my heart when I had no idea what it wanted? Most of the time, I just wanted to stay alive until tomorrow and not break my mother's heart by getting killed in the streets.

Miss Nixon got off the treadmill, downed a glass of water that was sitting on a nearby table, and sat on a chair across from me. We spent the next two hours talking about life, my family, her family, my journal, her career, and what life was like living in the Southeast DC housing projects. I wasn't used to sharing my feelings like that with anyone but my mom, but Miss Nixon was the real deal. That was about the only way I judged people: whether or not I could trust them, and I knew I could trust this thin, blond White woman. I asked her what it was like writing the stories and told her how much my mom loved them. She seemed happy about that.

Later that afternoon, Bob and his mom took me to a friend's house. The friend had teenage boys, and they invited me to play a game of football with them. I ran circles around those kids. "Don't mess with a boy from the hood," I joked with them.

The rest of the weekend passed pretty quickly. The Nixons took me out to dinner on Saturday night with their friends. I was the only Black person dining there, but it didn't bother me and didn't seem to bother anyone else. We mostly talked about the ECC work. On Sunday, everyone slept in and then spent most of the day eating, looking at the paper—only the sports section for me—and hanging around the house. When it came time for Bob and me to return to Southeast DC, Miss Nixon pulled me aside.

"Rodney, thank you for sharing your story with me," she said. "There's a certain light in you, and I know you are going to do great things."

I laughed. "I don't know about that, Miss Nixon."

"I do," she said. "I am an excellent judge of character, and I know you are headed for good and important things. Oh, and please call me Agnes."

She didn't judge me about the guns or the drug dealing or anything. She asked me to stay in touch with her, and I said I would. That was the start of a long—if unlikely—friendship.

I threw my backpack in the trunk of Bob's car, and we pulled out of the driveway. I was quiet on the way home, thinking about what Agnes Nixon had said to me. The cynical side of me thought, *This rich White lady has no clue about my life, so how can she say I'm gonna do big things?* And the thoughtful side of me—which I tried to press down like you would clothes in a drawer—thought, *This lady is smart and successful, maybe she* does *see something in me that I don't know yet.*

The thing was, hope in the future was something alien to kids like me growing up in the projects, surrounded by violence, drugs, guns, and poverty. Trying to hope for something was like trying to catch a butterfly: it was always just out of reach, and even if you were lucky enough to gently close your hand around its fluttering wings, it was so dang fragile that you knew it would never survive, and so you just had to let it go.

We headed into DC, and Bob dropped me off at my apartment.

"Thanks, man," I said, grabbing my backpack.

"See you tomorrow, Rodney?"

"Yup, see you tomorrow."

I opened the door to my apartment and dropped my backpack on the floor. I walked over to the box of guns, gave it a little kick, and then turned in for the night.

The next morning, I showed up at ECC as usual, checked in, pulled on my waders, and started pulling trash out of the Anacostia. Anthony was a few yards away. We glared at each other, but he didn't say a word, so I didn't have to shoot him.

That afternoon, Bob gathered the eight of us in a circle, and said he wanted to talk to us about something. I thought maybe Anthony and I were going to get fired for fighting, but I had it all wrong.

A few months earlier Bob had told us that he wanted our group to try and reintroduce the native bald eagle back to the Anacostia River. We thought that was cool, but didn't really think much more about it. That day, though, Bob started talking about it again, and said he was really serious. He told us that bald eagles used to practically rule the area around the Anacostia.

"What happened to them?" I asked. "Why did they leave?"

Bob said that eagles hadn't been seen around the Anacostia since the 1940s, primarily because of pesticides like DDT and pollution. In the years since then—as we knew—the Anacostia had just gotten dirtier and dirtier, becoming the trash-filled swamp we were trying so hard to clean up.

"Dang, no wonder those eagles said, 'Man, we ain't never going back to that dump,'" I said, and everyone laughed.

Bob said that now that we had made some progress in cleaning up the Anacostia, he could purchase several baby eagles—eaglets—from a place in Wisconsin, and our job would be to care for them until they became adults with the idea that they would mate, and we would slowly grow a brand-new population of bald eagles. It was an interesting proposition, for sure. If anyone could bring the eagles back, it would be us— this ragtag group of tough kids from the projects. We were finally starting to understand that we could do anything we set our minds to. We could actually make a difference with something.

By that time, the Lower Beaverdam Creek was almost completely trash-free, and we had moved on to clear the shoreline of several other nearby tributaries that flowed into the Anacostia. It was clean enough now that maybe even bald eagles would want to call the river home.

Even though it would be about a year before we'd be able to get all of the permissions and make the proper plans so we could safely bring four young eagles to DC, I couldn't wait to get involved. I wasn't ready to admit it to myself, but deep inside I wanted to be done with drugs and guns and stupid confrontations with Anthony. I was just drawn to being outside, like I always had been. I was ready to be up close and personal with bald eagles. I told Bob to count me in.

Chapter 6

"This is not a game. This is not a hobby. This is not just a sport. This is a whole new lifestyle for you."

This is what I say to Mike, at the beginning of his first falconry session. After reminiscing about the day I rescued Dippy, the juvenile eagle, from the clutches of a security fence, it's time to get down to business. Mike already has an overall sense of what falconry is about from watching me, but he has to know exactly what he's getting into. It's about so much more than just reading a manual and taking a test.

When someone commits to falconry, it can't be about ego, because ego always gets bored eventually and has to move on to the next shiny object in order to feed itself. As the manual says: "Park your ego at the front door," because you can't move on from falconry once you've made the commitment.

Mike and I walk into the building on my property that serves as an aviary but also as a place where I give presentations to kids and anyone interested in raptors. The front room is the demonstration area. About twenty chairs are set up in rows, and the walls are covered with photos, drawings, and paintings of birds that people have given me over the years, along with a few awards I've received. My loud-mouthed Harris's hawk named Chuck, after my late brother, is squawking from his aviary in the next room. Mike and I sit on chairs facing each other.

As I look at Mike's face, I have no doubt about his determination. When he sets his mind to something, he gets it done. I am confident that once he learns the basics, he will grow into a master falconer. I learned about my son's courage the summer when he was seven years old. It was a hot, sunny day, and Mike was at his aunt's house on Sixth Street SE, playing outside with friends. Some older kids had opened a fire hydrant, and everyone was playing in the whooshing water. This was the summer activity of choice when you were poor and growing up in the projects. That day, most of the kids saw a car coming down the street and jumped onto the sidewalk, but Mike was having so much fun splashing around that he didn't notice. The car hit Mike and sent him flying. He was conscious but was screaming in agony. Some of his teeth had been knocked out, and several bones were smashed, including his right femur.

I was visiting with an ECC member when I learned what had happened, and I rushed to Children's National Hospital on Michigan Avenue. Leaning over Mike's bed, I vowed to him and to myself that I would not leave him until he was completely healed. When he was finally released from the hospital in a body cast, Mike came to stay with me at my second-floor apartment on Martin Luther King Boulevard SE. On nice late-summer days, I would gently place him in a wheelchair and carry him down the stairs so he could sit outside in the sun. We talked a lot during that time, and I guess you could say our father–son bond grew stronger. When Mike finally got out of the cast, he basically had to learn how to walk and run again. Through that whole ordeal, he was always cheerful and never felt sorry for himself. Mike drew on all of his inner resources to recover, and it was hard not to be impressed by his sense of purpose. Now that he is a grown man and a father himself—and a firefighter at that—I'm certain he will bring that same tenacity to falconry.

"Okay, Mike, you already know some basics about falconry," I say. I want to make sure you understand the history and the legacy of this sport and art form."

I tell Mike that no one is certain of the exact year that falconry came into existence, but most experts agree that it started in the Middle East—Mesopotamia and the Arabian Gulf in particular—around four thousand years ago, maybe even longer. That blows my mind. When food was scarce, hunters realized they could train birds of prey to capture the food for them. Falconry eventually began to be considered a sport and an art, and it spread eastward and westward across the globe. Falconry really flourished in Russia, Turkey, and Kazakhstan, in particular.

When the sport moved to Europe sometime around the Middle Ages, it became an activity for royalty and those in leadership, primarily with falcons rather than hawks. Falcons give a clean, noble death to their prey before eating it, unlike hawks. Falcons primarily go after birds; their talons are made to snatch birds right out of the sky. And falcons have a small notch near the back of their beaks. When they capture a bird, they are able to fit its vertebrae neatly into that notch and break its neck. The bird is dead before the falcon even lands. The clean killing appealed to the royals. Oh, if those kings and princes could see me now, clomping around in my Timberlands, hunting my birds, and probably doing it better than they ever could. Mike laughs when I say this.

The global popularity of falconry took a nosedive between the sixteen hundreds and the eighteen hundreds, when firearm use increased and shooting became the new "in" sport.

There may have been some falconers among the European settlers who arrived in America in the early sixteen hundreds, but the Falconers' Association of North America was started in the early 1940s, when the United States had fewer than 200 falconers. Within a few years, though, the organization fell apart after World War II. Falconry in the United States took off again during the 1960s and has been growing ever since, along with what is now called the North American Falconers Association.

I pull a few books off my shelf so Mike can learn more about the history of falconry. This is nice, sitting here with Mike, talking about falconry, knowing that he is about to become part of something that is bigger than him in so many ways.

"Okay, next up is equipment," I say. "I know you've watched me a lot, flying my raptors and doing presentations, but you need to know your equipment inside and out. If not, it could result in an injured bird or worse, losing a bird, and trust me, you do not want that to happen."

I've laid out several pieces of equipment—some

falconers call it *furniture*—on a table in the presentation room. Today, I'm just going to review the most critical equipment.

"First up is the jess," I tell Mike, holding one up for him to see. "The three most important pieces of equipment are the jess, the swivel, and the leash, and they all work together."

The jess is a thin strap of leather that goes around a bird's ankle. Falconers use a jess to keep control of their bird when it is out of the aviary, on your glove, or if you are in the process of training it. Some falconers make their own jesses, and others buy them. I prefer to make my own, using kangaroo hide because it's thin but really strong and smooth. A jess can't be too tight or it could cut off circulation, but it can't be too loose either or the bird could slip its foot through the anklet and either fly away or break its leg. You have to oil the jesses about once a month so they stay supple.

The swivel is a metal clasp of sorts that goes between the jess and the leash. It's a small but critical piece of equipment because, without it, the leash will get tangled almost as soon as the bird starts to move. Swivels come in different sizes according to the type of bird it's being used on.

Various materials can be used for the leash, such as nylon or leather, and it's always a good idea to keep an extra one in your pocket. You can also make your own leashes with some durable climbing rope. The leash is clipped or tied to the falconer's glove, which is another piece of important equipment if you don't want your hand shredded by hawk talons. (I've been there, and it isn't pretty.) The slightest pressure of a raptor's talons can puncture human skin like a big pin in a pincushion. The glove should be leather, and—like the leash and jess—it's good to have an extra one.

"Listen, Goober," I say. "Falconry can be unpredictable, which is why you have to pay attention and be prepared. That's why I'm telling you to always have extras of your equipment on hand."

Just last week I was giving a presentation to a group of students with one of my red-tailed hawks, when the jess snapped in two. I thought I had treated the leather to the point of being supple enough, but I was wrong. I held the hawk down on the table, grabbed the extra jess from my pocket, and attached it to the talon. Problem solved—but if I hadn't had the extra jess in my pocket, the bird would have likely flown up to one of the rafters in the presentation room. Not the end of the world, but it would have interrupted the session with the kids and might have scared some of them.

Mike has worn one of my gloves before while holding a bird, but now he will need to find his own. A welder's glove is a good place for beginners to start.

Mike eventually needs to learn about other equipment as well such as scales and perches, but I want to talk to him about ethics.

"Ethics? Dad, c'mon, you know I'm an ethical person," says Mike.

"I know that, but falconry has its own code of ethics," I say. "For starters, most falconers are involved in conservation projects, because we've come to understand the deep connections between nature, animals, and humans."

Most falconers, at least the respectable ones, follow federal and state falconry laws. It might sound funny for someone with a past like mine to tell people to follow the law, but it's for the sake of the birds and the sport itself. Falconers must always do whatever is necessary to keep their birds healthy and fit, and if they can't commit to that, then it's time to give the birds to a falconer who will follow the code. Some raptors can live close to thirty years in captivity, so that's where the commitment comes in. They live almost twice as long as birds of prey in the wild.

"And it's the duty of every falconer who is sponsoring someone, like I'm sponsoring you, to pass on the code of ethics," I say.

Mike nods in agreement. "But when can I get a bird and let the fun stuff begin?"

I laugh. "The fun stuff? You're crazy," I say, but I know exactly what he means. He's talking about that feeling of freedom and peace you get when you fly your raptor, watch it soar overhead against the sky, land in a tree, and take off again to land on your glove and come home.

"Listen, there's something I haven't told you yet," I say. "You have to be prepared to get emotional."

"What do you mean, I'll 'get emotional'?" asks Mike. He's been taking some notes, but he stops.

"When you trap your first bird, and you hold it for the first time, you're gonna cry," I say. "You're holding this bird, and it's like you're wrapping all of nature in your arms, and you know your life is never going to be the same again. And the first time your bird comes to your glove, you cry again. Also, when you release your first bird. And when your first bird dies? Well, I'm warning you, Goober, you are going to cry like a baby."

Mike throws his head back in this way he does and laughs. "I don't know, Dad—that sounds like a lot of crying. That's you, but it might not be me."

"Okay, okay, we'll just see," I say. "We shall see."

The rest of the afternoon I spend explaining to Mike the other things he has to do to prepare for the test, such as learn about the different types of raptors, the rest of the equipment, health issues that birds might have, hunting techniques, and the local and federal regulations. Before anyone can even think about flying a bird—"the fun stuff"—they have to take a test and get approved to be an apprentice.

I pick up a copy of the *California Hawking Club Apprentice Study Guide*, which accompanies the manual, and I shake it at him.

"You have to know this book inside and out," I tell Mike. "It's not like high school. You need to get 80 percent on that test, or you can't practice as an apprentice, and you have to wait a month before you can take the test again."

This is where the determination part comes in. Taking that test and getting the license is only the first step. Once Mike becomes an apprentice, he has about two years of work ahead of him, training with one of my birds so he knows what he's doing, learning how to build an aviary, getting it inspected, and trapping his first bird. Falconers have to trap a bird from the wild within their first year of being an apprentice. We only trap juvenile birds, because those are the most at risk of dying. More than 75 percent of hawks die before they reach their first year, most hit by cars or trucks. By trapping juveniles, helping them survive through their first winter or two, and releasing them as adults, we are helping to grow the population when they might otherwise might not have made it to adulthood. So, for example, if the first bird Mike traps happens to be an adult, he will have to let it go and try again until he traps a juvenile.

"I want to do this, Dad," Mike says, looking through the guide.

"Well then, get ready to study your ass off," I say, laughing.

Mike and I walk into the aviary so he can think about which of my birds he wants to train with once he passes the test. There's Agnes—that bird is my heart—named after my friend Agnes Nixon. Agnes the bird is strong and wise, just like Agnes the woman. Mike walks around and looks at the rest of the gang: Joey, Gloria, Nanny, Squeal, and Chuck.

"Agnes," says Mike, without a shade of doubt in his voice. "There's something about her."

"Yep, there sure is," I say. "Agnes it is, then."

For about the next month Mike comes over for regular lessons with me, practices holding Agnes, studies the falconry guide, examines how I made my aviaries, takes the sample tests, and announces that he is ready to take the apprentice test. It's a multiple-choice test, and it's a little tricky, but I agree that Mike is ready.

We were both wrong.

My phone rings, and it's Mike.

"What's the word, Goob?"

"Dad, I got two answers wrong, and I got a seventy-seven."

"Okay," I say. "What are you gonna do about it?"

"I'm not upset that I failed," Mike says. "I need to try

harder. I know that. I can take the test again in thirty days, and that's what I'll do."

"Mike, falconry is about learning as you go," I say. "As long as you learn from your mistakes, then you'll continue to grow as a falconer. "

On the exact thirtieth day after Mike had taken the first test, he calls me.

"Dad, I'm on my way to take the test again," he says.

"All right, then," I say. "Pray to your grandmother. This might call for bringing out the big guns and asking Dippy to help you from heaven."

A few hours later my phone rings, and it's Mike. He sounds quiet and depressed, and I know what that means.

"Hey, Dad," he says.

"Hey, Goob—bad news about the test?"

"It was hard, Dad."

"I know it's hard, Mike," I say. "You'll have to wait another thirty days and try it again."

"No, I won't," he says.

I don't say a word, because I'm afraid he means that he is going to give up on falconry.

"I'm not taking the test again," he says, and pauses for a few seconds. "Because I passed with a perfect score! Ha ha ha, I had you going good, Dad."

"You devil," I say, laughing. "Making me think you were gonna quit."

"I'm not a quitter, Dad. I'm like you."

"You know what's next," I say.

"Yep, I have to build my aviary."

"That's right," I say. "And then the fun stuff begins."

"And then the fun stuff begins."

Chapter 7

"Yo, yo, yo," I called, running up the metal ramp to the old pump house and flinging open the door. "The eagles are coming, the eagles are coming."

Everyone laughed, and so did I. This was a big day for the Earth Conservation Corps and for all of us who had worked so hard to get to this point.

Bob Nixon had finally been given permits from the US Fish and Wildlife Service to bring four young eagles from Wisconsin to Southeast DC and place them in an artificial nest in a poplar tree on property owned by the National Arboretum. He was on his way from the airport, where he and a few members of our crew had gone to pick up the eagles. The rest of us were waiting at the pump house.

The Old Capitol Street Pump House is the office for

ECC, but it wasn't always that way. It was built in 1903 and was used to turn water from the Anacostia River into steam heat for the US Capitol. Over the decades, though, industry began to grow and pollution spread its dirty tentacles into the Anacostia and the air above, choking everything in its path. I imagined the pollution and poison of those years as a greenish, gaseous monster of sorts, wrapping its arms around Southeast DC and trying to smother us all. It almost succeeded.

The Anacostia became so sick with trash and pollution that the water couldn't even be turned into steam anymore. Think of what little effort it takes to put a kettle of water on the stove and heat it until steam comes up. Now imagine water so slogged down with debris and slime that steam can't even rise out of it. That's why, around 1950, the Old Capitol Street Pump House was abandoned, and there it sat, home to only die-hard weeds and whatever trash would blow into it.

In 1993, Bob Nixon showed the city all of the amazing work our team was doing, and he convinced them to give the pump house to ECC. Clearing away decades of brush and renovating the decrepit pump house into our office was a bit much, even for our dogged group, so we partnered with some area corporations and community organizations that donated supplies and volunteers. The word was starting to spread about the difference we were making, and people wanted to be part of our efforts. That was fine with us. We could use all the help that came our way. It felt a little strange having an actual office, because the Anacostia River had been the only office we knew, but it also made us feel like we were finally legit.

"They're here," someone shouted. Bob pulled the van up to the pump house and we ran out to the narrow ramp that we called "the catwalk." He unlocked the back of the van and pulled out two dog carriers, each with two young eagles in it. I was straining to get a look.

The eaglets were about two months old and had come from a sanctuary in Wisconsin. Generally, adult female eagles lay one, two, or three eggs. Sometimes the mother pushes the smallest egg out of the nest because she thinks it won't survive. That's some tough love, all right. The sanctuary in Wisconsin rescues those eggs and incubates them in nests made by humans but designed to feel and look like real eagles' nests. When the eaglets hatch, the rescuers use a puppet made to look like an eagle to feed them. When the eagles grow to between two and three months, they're sent to people like us, who are trying to grow the population of bald eagles.

Eagles have been off the endangered species list since 1997 and have made a remarkable comeback in many US states, especially Wisconsin. They had been put on the endangered list in the 1970s, when heavy pesticide use and human carelessness and indifference (what else is new?) practically wiped out this natural treasure. Over the years, DDT was banned, federal and state laws protecting endangered species were enacted, and public awareness grew thanks to innovations like nest cams, and the bald eagle made its comeback. I was proud to be part of an effort to bring the bald eagle back to the nation's capital.

I peered into the crates and was surprised to see that the young eagles just looked like big brown birds. Where were the golden beaks and the powerful white heads? Bob explained that eagles go through several phases when they are growing and that it takes four to five years for them to become adults. In the first phase—which these young dudes were still in—they have dark heads, dark feathers, and their bellies are white with some brown spots. The juvenile eagles enter the next phase in their second and third years. During this time their bellies become mostly white but still have some brown flecks, and their heads and feathers are still dark. Once they reach adulthood, their beaks turn that well-known golden yellow and their heads become snowy white. It was hard for me to imagine that these rug rats would one day turn into mighty bald eagles.

Now came the hard part: we had to hoist the hack box—the artificial nest—up into the tree we had chosen and then get the young eagles into it.

Hacking is the method used to simulate a natural eagle's nest by using an artificial nesting tower. Eagles generally return to the area where they were raised and fledged—or at least within seventy-five miles of it—when they are mature and ready to reproduce. Eagles' nests have sticks around the edges and soft material such as moss or plant leaves inside on the floor of the nest. The idea behind hacking is to make the eaglets think they are in a real nest and being fed by their parents. If all goes as planned, once our young eagles reach adulthood, they will stay in the same general area and hatch their eggs. That's how we would slowly build up the population.

We had hired a contractor to make the hack box and the nest inside so that we could be sure we had the exact dimensions and materials that would work. The outer box had a door so we could put the eagles inside and release them when we were ready. It had slats along the top where we would drop in food for them.

We grabbed some tools and other materials, put the eagles back in Bob's van, and climbed in the back with them. Waiting for us at the site was one of the partners who had helped us with the pump house renovation and who had agreed to lend us a cherry picker.

Using a clothesline pulley system, we hoisted the hack box up into the air until it was near the top of the tree. Our buddy with the cherry picker helped secure it between branches. Then we sent the pet carriers up the pulley, one at a time. Finally, the eagles were in the nest and the hack box door was shut. This had to happen quickly, because the idea was not to let the young eagles see any humans so they wouldn't imprint on us or identify with us as a species. They don't break out of the egg knowing who they are; they have to learn that they are mighty eagles, not goofy humans.

We quietly high-fived one another once the eagles were safely in their nest. We were exhausted, but the day's work wasn't finished yet.

Anthony and Burrell volunteered to do the first feeding. We had bought some freshly caught fish, and Anthony and Burrell took the fish out of a cooler and put them in a bucket. The rest of us watched from a small clearing in the woods as they secured the bucket to the pulley and slowly hoisted it up to the hack box, being careful not to spill any. Once the bucket was hovering above the hack box, they had to pull on a rope attached to the system, tipping the bucket and dropping the food into the eagles' mouths so they thought it was coming from their mother. It was a hard job that required precision and patience.

After the eagles had had their first meal in the hack box, we stood silently in the woods for a few minutes and just looked at one another. This was a solemn moment. Even before the eagles arrived, we had decided as a group that we would name one of them Monique, after our murdered crew member. We felt her spirit among the trees that day, like she was cheering us on, and we all cried, even me and Anthony.

We took turns feeding the juvenile eagles. Tink fed the eagles as well, but he volunteered to also fill in the logbook with information about the birds such as what time they were fed, what they ate, and any activity he observed. I didn't have the patience for that. Tink would sit for hours observing the eagles and making notations in the logbook. All of this continued for about two months, until it was finally time to set them free.

We were nervous, and we knew it would take time. It's not like we would just open the door and watch the four eagles flying off majestically into the sunset, like some Disney movie. Juvenile eagles don't just take off and start flying. They have to learn. Like humans: we crawl first and then comes our walking and running. Eagles engage in a process called *branching*. For several weeks they hop from branch to branch in their home tree. They flap their wings a few times to test them out, like kicking the tires on a new car.

From our hidden spot in the woods, we watched our eagles start branching. More than once we had to cover our mouths to keep from laughing out loud, because the eagles were so goofy. One flapped its wings and then awkwardly stumbled to the next branch below. Like when a baby starts to walk, he sways back and forth, tries to take the next step, but instead falls on his butt.

For the next two to three weeks we continued to sneak fish into the nest, until all four started flying. Once they had the flying part down, they would be able to hunt on their own.

Maybe this eagle reintroduction thing might work after all here on the Anacostia, I thought. I imagined how, maybe in several years, eagles would be a regular part of the wildlife in Southeast DC. And it would be because of us.

I had never been a part of something so amazing in my life, and I was learning that nature in general is complex and simple at the same time. Complex because it can be so hard for us to imitate it—like with making the hacking box, but simple because life just keeps happening over and over, and because nature is resilient. That is how I felt some days: tough and resilient. In spite of everything that had happened to me, like my father being murdered when I was fifteen, me getting shot at in a drive-by, seeing friends killed by rival gunfire, watching men I knew hauled off to jail, I was still here. Like those young eagles—still here. I was learning what resilience really meant.

Around the same time that we were releasing the eagles, Bob Nixon had started bringing some injured raptors to ECC. Since the birds would never be able to fly again, Bob had the idea that we could care for them and eventually use them to teach people about the lives of raptors and why places like the Anacostia were so critical to their survival.

The first bird I ever held was one of those injured raptors—a Eurasian eagle-owl named Mr. Hoots. He was a resident entertainer of sorts at one of those big amusement parks. When one of Mr. Hoots' wings was injured, the park didn't want him anymore and so he came to us. The first day Mr. Hoots arrived, I was there, and Bob, a full-fledged falconer, showed me how to hold him. I pulled on the protective glove, and Mr. Hoots hopped onto it. I was mesmerized. He was only about four pounds, but he was large, with a wingspan of about six feet. He turned his head from side to side and for a second I thought he might turn his head in a full circle. Then Mr. Hoots looked at me with his deep, burnt-orange eyes, and I felt something tug at my soul, like when I'm fishing and I get a bite. When I gave Mr. Hoots back to Bob, I felt empty, as though I had just let a piece of myself go. So many new things were coming my way, but I wasn't sure how to digest it all. My connection with Mr. Hoots and witnessing the young eagles made me wonder what else was out there for me to discover.

Those eaglets weren't the only babies in my life. I already had two kids, Rodney Jr.—aka Little

Rodney—and Shenika, and I had recently learned that I also had a three-year-old son, Mike. I was happy to learn about Mike and add him to the clan. By this time, the Anacostia River was becoming a part of my identity. I wanted to share my recent discoveries with my kids and show them that adventure and thrills can be found in nature rather than in the streets. I'd often bring my children to ECC to help us pull trash out of the river and to learn about birds. They loved it, and my ECC buddies welcomed them to the Anacostia family. My children, especially little Mike, loved running around near the water and looking for wildlife.

Don't get me wrong, though. Being a father and having that experience with Mr. Hoots and the eaglets still didn't give me some big come-to-Jesus moment. I knew I was becoming part of something bigger than myself, but I was still in my twenties. Even though I might have had one foot in ECC, the other foot was still firmly planted on the streets of Southeast DC. I was working on the Anacostia during the day and hustling drugs around apartment complexes and projects like Valley Green at night. Still running from the cops, still seeing people I knew get shot. I kept expecting my life to change somehow—maybe I'd stop being so reckless—even though I was doing the same crap every night.

My older brother Chuck and I were hanging out a lot—he was hustling coke as well. He had a connection in New York, and he was buying some really good dope. We were in business together and making great money. In some ways, Chuck was like the father I never had. He was three years older than me, and he would give me advice about all sorts of things and try to make sure I was safe. He stopped hustling before I did, because he became interested in playing semi-pro football. But Chuck was always supportive of me, even when I was doing the wrong thing. We were just tight.

The main thing that started bothering me wasn't that I might get shot and killed—that was pretty much a given—but the penalties for drug dealing were getting heavier. Mandatory minimum sentences were being put into play, and I could go to prison for a long time for even a small amount of coke. I couldn't risk that, not with small kids and the work we were doing at ECC.

I started thinking that maybe it was time to change up my hustle a little. I could move away from selling coke, and eventually just sell weed. The market for marijuana was growing bigger, so, according to my calculations, I could make almost as much as I was making by selling coke. I had several part-time jobs, such as driving a food delivery truck, in addition to ECC, and almost all of my co-workers at those jobs smoked, so they would happily be my clients, and I would be less likely to go to jail for selling weed.

I told Chuck about redirecting my hustle. He thought it was a good idea, and he gave me a bong with an image of the Grim Reaper on it to celebrate my new business. I loved it.

My plan worked for a few years, except for one unexpected problem: unlike with coke, I was selling weed to more and more people who knew me and knew where I lived. More people who knew I was dealing meant I was running a greater risk. One of my customers got arrested and, hoping to catch a break for whatever crime he had committed, he snitched on me. He insisted to the cops that I was a high-level dealer, selling all kinds of drugs. That interested the cops, and they came to get me.

Chapter 8

2017

Now that Mike has passed his test, he is a full-on falconry apprentice. I have already started teaching him how to hold Agnes, and today he is going to learn how to fly her.

"Dad, I'm so happy to be doing this," Mike says.

"This is just the beginning of the journey," I say.

According to guidelines issued by the North American Falconers Association, now that Mike has passed the initial falconry test, he has one year to build an aviary, get it inspected and approved by inspectors from the fish and wildlife offices of the Maryland Department of Natural Resources, and trap his first bird.

I know Mike has what it takes to get to the general and master levels of falconry; after all, he had the

determination to go through the process of becoming a DC firefighter.

About six years ago, Mike decided he wanted to apply to be a firefighter. He had always been drawn to the profession. When he was a kid, he watched a fire crew come and put out a fire in the neighborhood, and he started talking to one of the firemen. After that, he was hooked.

There was a time when we thought Mike might not be able to follow his dream. Part of becoming a firefighter is that an applicant also has to undergo training to become an emergency medical technician. Mike was struggling with his studies for the EMT testing.

"It's so hard," Mike told me.

"Well," I said. "If you can't give it your all, then don't do it."

Mike went over to see Dippy about whether or not to keep going or to quit.

"Grandma, it is so hard. I don't know if I can do it," Mike said to my mom, describing the challenging EMT test.

Mike wasn't sure if she really understood what he was talking about because she was in the kitchen standing at the sink, washing and drying dishes, and putting them away. She didn't say much about the EMT test. They talked for a little while about Mike's children, and then Mike said he had to get home.

He kissed his grandmother on the cheek and opened the front door of the apartment to leave.

"Oh, Mike?" Dippy called. "Don't come back here without that EMT license."

That's how my mom was. You'd think she wasn't

really paying attention, but then she would say some-thing to you and it's like *BAM!* She was listening and thinking the whole time, and when you weren't expect-ing it, she would lay some deep message on you.

Mike went home, decided he hadn't given it his all, and set about studying again. The rest is history. My mom knew he could do it. Big Dippy knew. It's just that Mike didn't know.

And now, here he is starting another challenge: falconry.

Today I'm going to show Mike how to fly Agnes. I had built a separate aviary just for Agnes—it's large with several perches for her to fly to. Once you trap a raptor, the first thing you have to do is train it to sit on and then fly to your glove and start trusting you. Because Agnes has already bonded with me, this will be a little easier for Mike now than it will be when he trains his first wild bird, but it's still a good way for him to learn. Basically, it's the process of transforming a wild bird of prey into a reliable falconry hawk. The goal is to eventually be able to "hunt" your bird. That means that your hawk flies free and finds and captures its prey, but then comes back to you. Mike has a way to go before he gets to that point.

Every bird is different, and it can take anywhere from a few days to as long as a couple of weeks to gain its trust. Knowing that Mike will be training with Agnes,

I've withheld food from her for a little while, so she is good and hungry. When Mike arrives, he puts on the glove and moves toward her. She tilts her head and looks at him. Mike holds the glove out to her. Agnes hesitates for a second and then hops onto the glove. I've trained her to do that.

"It's going to take a little more time and patience on your part when you trap your first bird," I say. "When that happens, you have to spend a few days getting it used to hopping to the glove. Now what do you do next?"

"Feed her, of course," says Mike.

The only way to train and bond with a bird is by using a reward, and that reward is always food. Mike reaches into his pocket and pulls out one of the dead mice I've given him. He holds it out to Agnes, who seems to give him the side eye, like she's not sure she can trust him. I've had Agnes for six years, and we have a strong bond. I sometimes take her to presentations because she is docile, but she is not used to someone else feeding and flying her.

"Be patient," I tell Mike. "You're asking her to put her head down and take food, but that's a vulnerable position for her."

Mike raises his arm so Agnes will instinctively fly off and back to the perch, and then holds the glove out again so she can get used to flying to him. This time she flies right back to the glove, puts her head down, and grabs the mouse with her beak. Mike looks at me and smiles.

I explain to Mike that the idea is to step progressively away from the bird so it has to fly farther and farther to get to the glove, and keep doing that for several days. Once it starts getting used to the falconer and flying to the glove for food, it's time to practice outside.

Outdoor training starts by attaching a long, fifty-foot cord called a *creance* to the jess around the hawk's leg.

"Think of this as a series of steps," I explain to Mike. "First, your bird jumps a short distance, then it flies to the glove for a small bit of food. The food is always the reward, remember? If the bird doesn't fly to the glove or doesn't do what you want it to do, don't give it the reward. The important thing is that you let the hawk set the amount of time it takes to be trained."

Mike attaches the creance cord to the jess on Agnes' ankle and carries her outside.

"Look at my Agnes staying on your glove," I say. "Agnes, you are my heart."

Once outside, I show Mike how to get Agnes to fly to his glove from the length of the cord. Mike puts her on a tree stump and walks about twenty-five feet away. He holds out the glove with a mouse and makes a chirping sound. A whistle works, too.

Agnes looks directly at Mike, spreads her wings and

flies over to the glove. Mike carries Agnes back to the tree stump, and repeats the process a few more times.

Agnes has had enough to eat now, so today's lesson is done. In the coming days, I'll show Mike how to fly Agnes with and without a cord. But if she is no longer hungry, she won't cooperate. Good falconers weigh their birds regularly and record the weight in a logbook. It's important not to let them get too heavy during hunting season, but you don't want them starving, either. Every bird is different, and the falconer must know the bird's optimal flying weight.

"When the bird starts doing what you want it to do, it has probably reached its optimal flying weight," I tell Mike, as we walk Agnes back to the aviary. I show Mike my logbook for Agnes, including the columns where I record her daily weight, when she was fed, what she ate, and any other notes. Mike examines it and takes a picture of the columns with his phone.

"The next time you come, you can fly her," I say.

"Dad, how will I know when a hawk—one that I trap and train—will be ready to free fly?" says Mike.

It's a good question, and there is no set answer. Even now, I still get nervous when I free-fly a bird for the first time. Most falconers have lost a bird at one time or another, usually because they get overconfident in their abilities. That's why I constantly tell Mike to check his ego.

"Since I'm your sponsor, we'll make that decision together after you've trained your first bird," I say. "In the meantime, you'll practice with Agnes."

For the next week or so, Mike comes over to practice flying with Agnes. He is a natural at falconry, just like I knew he would be. He is now ready for the next step: building his aviary. Sometimes, this is when new falconers decide the sport just isn't for them, because they realize what a time commitment falconry can be. Aviaries—sometimes known as *weatherings*—must be built to certain specifications while keeping in mind precautions such as proper ventilation, comfort for the bird's talons, and the possibility of predators. Finally, the aviary must be inspected by officers from a state's Department of Natural Resources.

Mike has just about finished his training with Agnes. She feels comfortable flying to his glove for food, and he feels comfortable flying her.

A few days after one of his final lessons with Agnes, Mike calls me just as I'm passing out the last of the dead mice to my hawks and falcons, and of course to the Eurasian eagle-owl, Mr. Hoots.

"Hey, Goob, what's up?"

"Dad, I met this Amish man today, and he said he could build my aviary for me for a thousand bucks. That sounds like a really great price."

I don't say anything. I'm surprised and a little disappointed. That's not what falconry is about. It's not about paying someone else to do your work for you. Falconry is about putting your blood, sweat, and tears into your craft. It's not about taking an easy way out. How can you be dedicated to your birds when you're not even willing to take the time to build their home?

"Well, that's one option, I guess," I finally say.

"Yeah, he says he's built one before, and he knows how to do it so it'll pass inspection on the first try."

I'm silent again.

"Dad?"

"Yeah, yeah, I'm here," I say. I know he can tell by my voice that something is wrong. "What's the rush?"

"Well, I only have a year," says Mike.

"A year is a long time," I say. "How about this? What if I pick up the wood and supplies and help get you started."

Now it's Mike's turn to be quiet.

"You don't think I should hire the guy," he finally says.

"I didn't say that."

"Dang, I know what you're doing," Mike says, and he starts to laugh. "You're laying a guilt trip on me."

I bust out laughing as well. "Hey, I'm your sponsor," I say. "That's what I do."

"You're gonna teach me?"

"You already know what to do from studying," I say. "But I will definitely help you start the work." In truth, I can't wait to show Mike how to start building an aviary. Damn. My son is really going to be a falconer.

When Mike's next day off from the fire station arrives, I stack the wood, nails, tools, and other supplies in the back of my van and head over to his house in Waldorf, Maryland, about an hour away.

Mike's three kids, Ayden, Amina, and Journee, come tumbling out of the house as soon as I pull up.

"Pop Pop! Pop Pop!" They run over laughing and squealing. I try to pick up all three of them in a bear hug.

"You gonna help us build a big house for the big bird?" I ask.

"Yes, yes, yes," they say, clapping their hands and jumping up and down. "Big bird!" I'm sure they're thinking of the Sesame Street character, but I don't correct them.

Mike comes out of the house.

"You ready?" I ask.

"Let's do this," he says.

Aviaries can be different sizes, but I prefer eight feet by eight feet by eight feet. That is the ideal size for raptors such as red-tailed hawks and Harris's hawks, which are the types of birds Mike will likely be trapping. Even though some falconers prefer artificial turf or sand for their aviary floors, I prefer natural ground—dirt with only a little grass, if any. That is the closest to nature, and I want to preserve that.

For the next two days, Mike and I work to get the walls cut and secured. The kids help by handing us tools and keeping us company. We use basic plywood because it's inexpensive, easy to obtain, and only needs to be treated with some wood preservative. Metal hawk houses can get too hot in the summer and too cold in the winter. Cinderblock can also get too cold and can be too abrasive for the birds.

Federal regulations call for aviaries to have at least one window to give the bird fresh air, natural light, and an interesting view. It should be high so the bird can look out and feel safe but also out of sight. The window must have slats for air to get through.

Once we get the walls up, I decide it's time for me to leave and Mike to take over. I know he wants me to stay and help finish the whole thing, but Mike will feel a greater sense of pride and ownership if he finishes it by himself, and I want him to feel that.

A few days later, Mike calls to say he has finished the aviary and has scheduled an appointment to get it inspected. An individual state's fish and wildlife service has to inspect every raptor aviary to make sure it complies with regulations and is completely safe for the bird.

I drive over to Mike's on the day of the inspection, and when I pull up, he's sitting on the front porch, watching his kids toss a ball around in the yard.

"Hey, Goober," I call, getting out of the car and hugging the children.

"You just missed the inspector, Dad," Mike says. "He left about fifteen minutes ago."

Mike looked down at his hands and then up at me. "It didn't pass."

Turns out Mike's window had too many slats, and the inspector thought that it would let air in but wouldn't allow enough sunlight through.

"He also said my perches need to be natural tree branches," Mike says. "That was the other thing wrong."

Mike had gotten some wooden poles from the hardware store and put some artificial grass on them. He is learning.

"Aw, man, you can't let that get to you," I say, noticing that Mike looks disappointed about not passing the inspection. "I've told you before, failure is the best teacher. Now you know what needs to be fixed, and you'll never make that mistake again. It's like Dippy used to say: 'You can have five minutes to feel sorry for yourself, and then you have to get back in the game.'"

Mike smiles. "I'll make the fixes this weekend and set a time for another inspection."

Soon Mike's first aviary passes the next inspection, and now all he needs is a bird to live in it. We decide to try and trap a hawk on the property where I live in Laurel, Maryland. I've seen all kinds of hawks and wildlife since I've been living there. The land is tree-covered and has little human population.

It's a cold but sunny morning when Mike arrives. We've already constructed the trap. I use what is called a *bal-chatri trap*, which was invented by falconers during the 1800s. Some say it means "small umbrella" because of the trap's shape, but others say it translates to "hair umbrella" because early users made them with horsehair. Today, falconers can buy bal-chatri traps, but as with most things, if I can make it myself, that's what I prefer to do. I use wire mesh to make the dome-shaped cage, and then I attach several nooses that I make with fishing string. When the raptor dives down to get the prey in the trap, the nooses catch its talons so the bird can't escape. The trap looks kind of messy, but it works like a charm. Mike and I built the trap we're using today, so he will know how to make his own in the future.

Mike carries a box with three live mice in it and a plastic pet carrier. I carry the bal-chatri, anklets, a jess, and a towel, and into the woods we go, our footsteps crackling on dried leaves and branches.

"You know, Goober, it's not unusual for it to take

several hours or even days to trap your first bird," I say, my warm breath making steam when it hits the cold air.

"I'm patient," he says. "I learned that from you."

We're barely in the woods for twenty minutes, when I stop short. Several yards away, in the lower branches of a tree sits a red-shouldered hawk, scanning the forest floor for a morsel.

"You know what that is," I whisper, pointing to the hawk.

Mike tilts his head and looks at the bird. "A red-shouldered hawk?" he says.

I slap his back with pride.

Red-shouldered hawks aren't exactly plentiful, but they aren't rare either. Medium-sized hawks, they are native to eastern North America and can also be found along the California coast. They're named for the reddish feathers around their neck, wings, and underside. If they stay healthy, they can live as long as twenty years.

I can't believe we've come across a hawk this soon. "Okay, you know what to do," I say.

I watch as Mike sets out the trap. He pulls out the box and dumps the three mice into the trap, where they start racing back and forth looking for a place to hide. Mike straightens out the nooses, and we walk backward about ten yards and hide behind a fir tree.

The hawk is still sitting on the branch, and now the three skittering mice have captured its attention.

"I think it's a juvenile female," Mike whispers, peeking out from around the branches.

Suddenly, the hawk dives down onto the trap. She realizes she is caught, but the more she struggles, the more the small nooses tighten around her thin legs. We have to work fast now.

Mike grabs the towel from me, puts it over her wings with one hand, while gently trying to undo the nooses from around her squirming talons and legs.

"Easy does it, easy does it," I say, noticing that Mike's hands are shaking. "You got this. Slow and steady. You don't want to hurt her. Just like the doctors say: first, do no harm."

Mike releases her from the trap. Two of the mice run out, and she has already killed the third with one of her sharp talons. I put the dead mouse in my pocket so Mike can feed it to her later. I hold the hawk wrapped in the towel while Mike puts anklets and jesses on her. Then I gently shove her in the carrier and shut the door.

Mike is breathing heavily and falls back onto the ground. I laugh.

"You doing all right there, Goob?"

"Dad, my heart feels like it's gonna come crashing right out of my chest," he says, sitting up.

"Let's get this girl back home and weigh her," I say. "Congratulations, son. You got your first bird."

Mike puts his head in his hands. He is crying.

"Remember when I told you how emotional it is when you trap your first bird, and you said you didn't believe that? Well, come on now, crybaby," I tease. "Let's go."

"It's overwhelming," Mike says as we walk back, with the hawk squawking and complaining in the carrier.

We return to the storeroom where I keep my scales, weigh her, and then return her to the carrier a second time. Mike puts the carrier in the back seat of his car and heads home to show his kids the hawk and get her settled in the new aviary.

I watch until his car is out of sight.

The next morning Mike calls to say the hawk isn't eating.

"Give her time," I say. "When she's hungry she will eat. Do you have a name for her yet?"

Mike doesn't say anything for a few seconds. "Yes, we have a name. She is Gorgeous Isabella Flowers."

I bust out laughing. "That's quite a name," I say. "I'm guessing you had a little help in naming her."

"Oh yeah," Mike says. "The kids love her."

About a month after Mike trapped her, Gorgeous Isabella Flowers stops eating. It turns out she has been carrying a deadly parasite. Mike is giving her medicine from the vet, but the outlook isn't good. When my phone rings at midnight and I see that it's Mike calling,

I have a bad feeling.

"Hey, Mike," I say.

"She's gone, Dad," says Mike, his voice cracking.

"Damn it," I say. "You did everything you could. You can't blame yourself."

"I know, but I didn't think I'd get so attached to her in such a short time," he says. "And the kids did, too. They pretty much cried themselves to sleep tonight."

"I have an idea," I say. "It's supposed to be cold but nice and sunny tomorrow. Bring the kids over, and we'll fly Agnes. It will take all your minds off of Gorgeous."

"I don't know, Dad."

"Look, you can all sit home and feel sorry for yourselves, or you can come over and find joy in the circle of life with me and Agnes," I say. "It's up to you."

"Okay, okay, we'll come over."

"There you go," I say. "That's more like it. And we'll talk about when to try and trap your next bird. You have to keep going."

"Dad, you were really right about the emotional side of falconry," Mike says.

"I know," I say. "I'm always right."

That makes Mike laugh, and we say goodnight.

And so the journey of our falconry family continues.

Chapter 9

2002

Shenika and Little Rodney were in the bedroom playing in the apartment I was renting on Martin Luther King Jr. Boulevard. Little bursts of laughter occasionally turned into higher-pitched whines of "Stop, I'm gonna tell Daddy," but nothing I had to intervene in. I was in the living room, half watching television and half making notes about how to divide the pound of marijuana I planned to sell that week. My other kids, Mike and twins, Diamond and Daisha, were with their moms.

It was close to nine o'clock, and my mom would be arriving soon from her Bible study class to pick up Shenika and Little Rodney to spend the night with her. The relative quiet in the apartment was suddenly broken by men shouting and banging on the door.

"Open up! Open the door! We got you! We got you now!"

"Aw, shit," I said, scrambling to hide the weed in an old cigar box on top of the television. "Rodney, Nika, get in here now."

My front door was being hit with some kind of club or battering ram, and they kept shouting.

Just as Rodney and Shenika came running into the living room, the door broke open, and about fifteen cops stormed into the apartment, guns drawn. Even though I made no move to resist, three of them grabbed me, pushed me on the floor on my stomach, and slapped handcuffs on my wrists. The rest of them had already started searching the apartment.

I asked if they had a warrant, and they did. I started to protest, but I knew they had me. They found the weed in seconds—I should have had a back-up plan for hiding it in a hurry. Shenika and Little Rodney sat silently, side by side on the couch, their skinny arms entwined. Shenika started to cry. Little Rodney looked at me, looked at his sister, and tears began to fill his big brown eyes, soon spilling down his cheeks.

"Look, you guys," I said, trying to sound as normal and calm as possible while a bunch of cops were rummaging through the apartment. The cops let me sit up. "You don't need to cry. It's going to be all right.

Grandma's on her way here to get you. Everything's gonna be okay. I promise."

In spite of what I had just said, inside I wasn't really sure that everything was going to be okay. I just couldn't stand seeing Shenika and Little Rodney crying with me sitting on the living floor in handcuffs, powerless, and unable to reach out and hug them. I was humiliated, angry, and, to be honest, a little scared. I had made it through more than a decade of hustling, never once being behind bars. Sure, over the years I had had run-ins with the cops, especially with DC's notorious "jump-out boys." They were DC cops who would send someone in undercover to buy coke from a street dealer. Once the cop bought the dope, a swarm of unmarked cop cars would pull up and surround anyone who was nearby. We'd start to run, but they would jump out, chase us, and beat the stuffing out of us. If they found drugs, they would take the drugs and plant them on someone they wanted to catch. It didn't matter whether we had been part of the original "buy bust" or not. I had a few tricks to get around the jump-out boys in case I was carrying when they pulled one of their stunts. I used to keep a small bag of potato chips on me, and if the jump-out boys started causing chaos, I'd stash the dope in the bag of chips, crumple the bag, and toss it. Even if they found it, they couldn't connect it to me.

That's one reason why, even though they arrested me several times, the charges could never stick.

I had stopped selling coke because the penalties had become so stiff, but the laws had recently changed for weed as well. Possession of any amount of marijuana over half a pound was a felony. I had a pound, so I was screwed. Fortunately, I had gotten rid of my guns when I stopped selling coke, so all the cops could take was my weed and my passport.

The two cops who had knocked me down now pulled me to my feet and—one on either side of me, walked me out of the apartment, each grabbing an arm. Like, where was I going to go? I could still hear my kids crying and calling me as the cops led me out.

From the back seat of the cop car, I saw my mom pull up, assess the situation, and run inside. At least now I knew my kids were safe. I would call Dippy when I got to jail, but I knew she would be worried and disappointed.

We arrived at the Central Detention Facility, also known as the DC Jail, where I was processed and put in an interrogation room, still handcuffed. A detective came in, introduced himself, and sat down across from me.

"Do you want to help yourself," he asked me. "Because you know you can make this really easy for yourself if you tell me where you got the weed."

"I bought it on the street," I said.

"You can't get that much weight on the street."

I didn't say anything.

"You mean to tell me that you are willing to take this rap all by yourself and do maybe five years?" he asked, putting his hands on the table and leaning toward me.

I still said nothing. No way would I ever snitch on anyone, even though I was pretty sure someone had done it to me. That is the number-one code of the street, and it was still the code I was living by.

The cop took me to a holding cell, where I spent the night. I was released the next day, after a court date was set for August, five months away. In the meantime, I wasn't allowed to leave the country, and I had to take a weekly urine test.

When the August court date arrived, I took a plea deal and was given a given a two-year sentence with all but 120 days suspended. I would be on probation for two years once I was released. I was instructed to turn myself in to DC Jail on September 10, which I did. A guard immediately put me in a cell, and I ended up staying there for a month while they looked for a more permanent facility for me.

I walked into DC Jail with an attitude. Even though I had never been locked up, I knew that I had to walk, talk, and act a certain way. The second another inmate saw even a small crack in my armor, they would squeeze in there and take advantage of me. I wasn't about to let that happen. I wasn't nervous, but I prepared myself for trouble to find me, which it did. I ended up fighting with some dude my first night behind bars.

The prison guards had put me in a two-person cell by myself because the other guy had been released. I was sitting on my bunk thinking about my situation. I was pissed at myself for getting caught with the weed. This big, bulked-up prisoner walked by and stopped at the bars of my cell. I just gave him a blank stare. He looked right back at me with no expression on his face. I could tell he was older because of his wiry gray hair and wrinkles crawling out from the sides of his eyes, but obviously he spent his days working out.

"You need to give me those other covers and pillow," he said in a raspy voice, pointing to the empty bunk. His forearm was about the size of my thigh.

I stood up and walked closer to the bars. "No, man," I said. "That's not happening. The blanket's in my cell, and that means it's for my use. Sorry, bro."

Fast as a racecar in the Indy 500, he reached in and grabbed my T-shirt, pulling me toward the bars. I started pushing him and I punched his wrist. He let go.

"When the doors pop," he said in a slow, low voice, referring to when the cell doors are unlocked.

"It's gonna be me. And you." He shook his head and walked away.

I was downright skinny compared to him, but I started doing push-ups on my cell floor, wondering how many I'd have to do until I was strong enough to bring him down.

"Yo, Slim," a voice called. It was a dude in the cell across from me. "You did the right thing. You can't ever give in to them."

The big guy returned a few hours later and stood at my cell door again.

He rubbed his chin and said, "Apologize."

"What?" I said. This time I stayed seated on my bunk.

"Apologize," he repeated.

"Naw, man," I said. "I ain't apologizing. You were the one who came up to me."

I stood up—at a safer distance away this time—and stared at him. He shook his head again and walked away.

"Slim, I'm glad you didn't apologize," said the prisoner across the hall. "That wouldn't have been a good look for you."

About an hour later, the muscular old guy comes back a third time. I thought, "This dude must really be out to get me."

I stood up and just stared at him.

"Listen, man," he said. "When these doors pop, you don't say nothing to me and I don't say nothing to you, got it?"

I didn't say a word, just slowly nodded my head. This guy could have crushed me, and I had no idea why he changed his mind, but I was glad he did. I didn't want to die over some stupid sheets.

The next day at breakfast I saw my cousin, who was also incarcerated in DC Jail. I told him what had happened the night before. My cousin was a Muslim, and he encouraged me to go to a prayer service with him. He said it was better to focus on that rather than fighting some guy who was almost twice my size.

I had never been to a Muslim service, but decided to go to see what it was all about. I sat next to my cousin and looked around the crowded room while waiting for the service to begin. That's when I saw him—the big prisoner who wanted to fight me.

I grabbed my cousin's arm. "Cuz, cuz, there's the dude who came to my cell." I nodded toward him. My cousin looked and then his eyes widened.

"Oh, man," he whispered. "That cat is in for murder. You know some of these lifers, they come in here as skinny as you, but year after year they do pushups and work out, and then they can do some major damage."

At that moment I realized that I would have to spend every single second in that place watching my back.

The big Muslim guy never came back to my cell, but I unknowingly flirted with trouble again a few days later. In jail, unspoken rules dictate every aspect of life, even when it comes to simple things like using the phone or standing in line for food.

I wanted to make a phone call and didn't realize that someone who was in line was holding the place for his buddy who was playing basketball. He wasn't using the phone so I jumped in front of him in line. The guy holding the place and I started to have words.

"Look man, when I gotta use the phone, I gotta use the phone," I said.

My cousin was several yards away and saw that I about to get into a brawl. He came over and pulled me away.

"Cuz, cuz, cuz," he said, holding my arm. "You got to understand that there is a different code in here. I have to tell you about jail etiquette so you don't end up getting both of us killed. You have to pick your battles, and trust me, bro, you don't want to fight over a stupid phone call. The consequences aren't worth it."

He sat me down and explained to me about prisoner hierarchy. I hated all of this bullshit. I just wanted to be back at ECC, working on the Anacostia and setting eagles free. Of course, they might never even take me back now that I had gotten arrested.

I started thinking a lot about my current situation, my life, and how I ended up here. One thing I had always told my children was that they had to have a plan for whatever they wanted to achieve in life. I would say to them, "If you don't have a plan, you've already failed." Now here I was, without a plan for my whole dang life. I felt like a giant wave—big, strong, and threatening—until it crashes into nothing.

It was my own fault; I couldn't blame the punk who snitched on me. I've never been the type of person to blame other people or situations for what I had done. People can put a crutch on anything if it means they don't have to take responsibility. That wasn't me. I owned up to every decision I've ever made. I just didn't know where my life would go after jail. The one thing I knew was that my body might have been locked up, but my mind wasn't. I knew that if I could depend on the power of my mind and my inner resources, then the path for my life would reveal itself to me. I just had to stay focused and away from all the prison nonsense. These were the thoughts swirling around my mind, like the murky waters of the Anacostia, and I would have given anything to be back on its banks right then.

One morning, I was sitting on the bunk in my cell, and I heard the solemn chants of the Muslim call to prayer. My cousin had told me that Muslims must pray in groups five times a day to praise Allah, to listen, and to leave the material world behind for that period of time. Some prisons and jails allowed group prayer and others didn't. At DC Jail, I heard the call to prayer every day; it wasn't unusual for incarcerated men to turn to the Muslim faith. That morning, something about the call to prayer made its way into my heart and my mind, and I started to cry. And I mean crying like a baby. I couldn't stop. Wiping away my tears with the back of my hand, I started to have a vision in my head. I was sitting cross-legged on a beach, feeling totally relaxed. No people were around, just the sound of waves hitting the shore and the occasional plaintive cries of seagulls. These waves didn't crash into nothingness; they receded back into the ocean to build up again. No bars surrounded me, just earth and sky. Earth and sky, sun and sea. At that moment, I felt surrounded by peace, and all of the weight lifted from my soul. The feeling that cinderblocks were attached to my legs melted away, and I had the sensation of floating. Weightlessness. Suddenly, a sense of clarity about my life that I hadn't felt in years—at least not since I was a kid, playing hooky to visit the big birds at the zoo—became evident to me. It was up to me as to whether or not to embrace it.

I can't explain what happened to me that morning, but afterward, I was different. This time, I really believed that everything was going to be okay. Maybe not that day, or the day after, but in time. I started attending the Muslim services at DC Jail, not because I had suddenly found religion—although I know some prisoners do—but because the services helped me hang on to this new sense of peace and direction.

I remained incarcerated at DC Jail for about six weeks, and then, over the next four months, I was moved to three different facilities, finally ending up at the Federal Correctional Institution in Morgantown, West Virginia. Each time I was moved to a new facility I was strip-searched. Nothing is more humiliating and demeaning then bending over for the strip search. You'd think by now they would have come up with some kind of X-ray or machine that could make that check. Then again, I suppose demoralizing the inmates is all part of the game.

When the security van dropped me off at Morgantown, snow was falling, and it snowed for the next eight days. It was a minimum-security facility and, being so close to getting out, I just kept my head down and stayed out of trouble. I was released on January 7, 2003, with a ticket for a Greyhound bus to drop me off back in DC. The bus broke down on the way, and I felt that old familiar anger start to bubble up, because I didn't think the bus driver was properly handling the situation. Anger used to be my go-to reaction in frustrating situations, along with taking everything personally, but I had made a commitment to change. This was going to take more time and effort than I realized, but I had no choice, unless I wanted to end up back in prison or worse.

I stayed calm and controlled my anger by cursing under my breath at the bus driver instead of getting into a fight with him. Eventually another Greyhound bus arrived, and we were on our way again.

My mom, Chuck, my two oldest children, and my girlfriend at the time—also a former ECC member—were waiting for me on K Street. We hugged and laughed, and I promised all of them I was never going back to jail. My mom looked a little skeptical, but my brother and kids cheered when I said it.

"I mean it, Dippy," I said, looking at my mom.

She nodded her head. "Well, you know, talk is cheap, so I guess you'll just have to show me."

I was out. Praise Allah—I was out. The nonstop noise of jail was still rattling around in my brain, and I craved to be outside in nature and alone. But I had nowhere to go but back to Southeast DC.

When I went to jail, I lost my former apartment on Martin Luther King Jr. Boulevard, so after my release I moved in with my girlfriend, who lived on Florida

Avenue. She and I had been dating for about the past year and a half. I knew I had to stay away from selling dope of any kind, but I needed to make a living. I was able to get several part-time jobs, including school bus driver, delivery driver for a wholesale meat company, and bouncer for Classics, a huge nightclub across from Andrews Air Force Base in Prince George's County. All those pushups I had done in jail had given me some bulk, so I was a good bouncer. I liked working at the meat company the best, because I was able to drive all over DC. I wasn't the kind of person who could sit still for very long, especially after being locked up, and being on the move felt good.

Fights were starting to break out at Classics on a regular basis, and I had a feeling it might get shut down soon, plus I didn't want to get in the middle of any fight if I could help it. Men would end up fighting over women or drugs, and a few shootings had happened there. One good thing about working at Classics was that my brother Chuck also had a job there, so we were able to look out for one another in case trouble started.

For about the next year and a half, I worked at all of my jobs and checked in regularly with my parole officer.

I would occasionally stop by ECC to greet the new employees, visit Bob Nixon and my friends who still worked there, and see my old friend—the Anacostia River. No one cared that I had been locked up—they only cared about whether I remained dedicated to wildlife and conservation. I still felt an empty space in my heart, but for the life of me I didn't know what belonged there. I kept trying to get back to that sense of clarity and peace that had embraced me during my vision at DC Jail.

One Thursday afternoon, I stopped by ECC before my shift at the nightclub, and the chief executive officer at the time, Glen O'Gilvie, came up to me. Although most members of our original crew had either died or left ECC, I still had some friends there, including my former enemy, Anthony.

"Hey, Rodney, good to see you," said Glen, slapping me on the back. "We need you back, man. Bad. Any interest? You can work with this new incoming corps. Today is their first day here." He gestured to a group of young people sitting on some picnic tables nearby. They were laughing and showing off for each other. One of the girls threw her head back and laughed at someone's joke. She reminded me a little bit of Monique.

"I'll do it," I said, and suddenly I felt like a weight had been lifted from my shoulders. I didn't even think about; I just knew it was what I should do.

"All right, that's great," Glen said, grinning. "You can start on Monday."

"This is the group I'll be training?" I asked, nodding my head toward the picnic tables. "Mind if I introduce myself now?"

"Sure, let's go," he said. I approached the group, and Glen explained who I was—he left out the jail part. I almost laughed, because these kids looked me up and down with the same know-it-all skepticism I had had toward Bob Nixon back on our first day at the Anacostia.

"Okay, y'all," I started. "As of Monday, I'm your new supervisor. You have two days to rest, because come Monday, I can promise you I will be kicking some butts."

I told them more about how I was part of the very first corps and about Monique and Tink and other corps members who had been killed. And I explained how they were going to learn aspects of the old Anacostia River that would make their heads spin.

"We don't want to lose any of you, so try to stay alive until Monday," I said, and then turned and headed out to my shift at Classics. In my head, I was already planning how the day would go on Monday and what I would teach the new corps members.

This would be the first time I would be on the teaching and directing side of the work at ECC, and it felt right. I knew exactly where these kids were coming from: broken homes, violence, drug-addicted parents, crappy schools, and the temptations of the streets. Maybe I had something to share. Maybe I could show them how nature and wildlife can save them, if they would just open their minds and let it all in.

Chapter 10

2004–2012

After meeting the new ECC corps group that Friday, I went to my shift at Classics and gave my two-week notice. I'd be making more money at ECC doing something I liked much better than working the door at a nightclub.

I returned to ECC and the banks of the Anacostia that following Monday. This would be the start of a five-year journey of teaching new corps members about the river, its native wildlife, and why they should care about conservation and the world around them. It felt good to be back, breathing in the air that was so much cleaner now, taking on new projects, observing the eagles that were now reproducing on their own, and just soaking up the space that is nature.

At first, it was a little strange to be on the teaching side of things, but it felt right. The young people respected me because they knew I was the real deal. I knew all their little tricks and games. Hell, I think I had even invented some of them. I also made it clear to corps members that I wouldn't stand for any bullshit. Disrespecting me was not allowed; that wouldn't work. Once we were all on the same page and knew who was who and what was what, we all got along. I was the alpha dog, and all these little pups knew they'd better not challenge me.

Every eleven months, a new corps group would be recruited from the surrounding neighborhoods. When meeting the incoming groups, I never had a memorized speech to give them or anything like that, but I made sure the message was clear. If they were serious about changing their lives, overcoming obstacles, opening their minds to something new, and thinking about their future, then this was a great opportunity for them. For many of them the word *future* was almost a foreign concept, just like it had been for me back then. Even though more than a decade had passed since our first ECC group formed, young people were still killing and getting killed in Southeast DC. Most of them started their work at the corps with the belief that they would not make it to age twenty-one, and many of them didn't.

One of the first murders of a person in my corps group happened on a Friday night and involved a second person from the corps. Everyone had just been paid and they were ready to party. They high-fived one another amid shouts of "See you Monday."

Two young men left ECC together and headed toward the house where one of them lived. Several other people joined them and were hanging out. A guy came over and started to pick a fight with one of the two corps members, accusing him of snitching on him for something he had done. Things got heated and the dude shot our corps member in the chest. According to witnesses, it was the other corps member who had provided the gun that killed the young member.

Word spread quickly among the corps members, and everyone was in a somber mood the next Monday, feeling the absence of the two young men and noting the unexpected betrayal. It's true that most of them already knew people who had been murdered, but this was more personal. They had worked with both of the young men, joked with them, eaten lunch together. Didn't that count for anything?

We all talked about it for a little while, but then I reminded them that we had work to do. Keeping them busy would stop them—at least for a few hours—from trying to make sense of the betrayal and the murder.

Environmental work never stops, because so much damage has been done. In the time since our original ECC group had been brought on board to clean

up much of the fourteen miles of the Lower Beaverdam Creek tributary, corps members have worked on
other conservation projects. The groups that I led were
involved in tree planting, restoration of shoreline plant
habitats, and water-pollution remediation. We would
also clear the way for trails that the city could turn into
river walks so people could start walking along parts of
the river.

Not all of the projects were rewarding for corps
members. Sometimes we would plan cleanups for
neighborhoods that bordered the Anacostia. We'd
meet at ECC, pack up trash bags, gloves, trash pickers,
rakes, and brooms, and get to work in the designated
neighborhood. Picking up stuff that other people had
thrown out was dirty work: used tissues, food wrappers,
chicken bones, dirty diapers, beer bottles—it could get
downright disgusting. We would tackle a five- or six-
block area, and divide and conquer. Two people would
clean up gutters, two others would sweep the sidewalks, and two others would cut down weeds choking
the sidewalks. Sometimes people would come out of
their apartments or stores and thank us, and we would
use that opportunity to talk to them about how dis-
carded trash ends up down sewers, eventually carried to
the Anacostia and the Chesapeake Bay, and ultimately
destroying our watersheds. Some said they had never
thought about it that way. There was a time when I

hadn't, either. I would toss empty cigarette packets and plastic Pepsi bottles out of my car window like it was nothing. That makes me cringe now.

At the end of a long day, after we had finished a particularly grueling neighborhood cleanup, the corps members and I sat back and surveyed our work.

"This looks good," one young man said, smiling. "Like, really good."

We went back to that same neighborhood about a week later only see the gutters and sidewalks covered with trash again. The corps members were utterly dejected. And mad.

"Man, why did we even bother?" said one girl.

"Look," I said. "People don't change their habits and their attitudes in one day or one week. You all probably know that better than anyone. But here's the thing: you now understand how this trash damages the entire planet, so it's up to you to teach other people. Your friends, your family. You have to pass on the knowledge—otherwise, what good is even having it?"

I don't know if I got through to them that day. I was disappointed too, but when people are living in poverty, maybe addicted to drugs, maybe homeless or hungry, they barely care about themselves, much less the world around them. No amount of trash cleaning is going to change those deeper, soul-crushing problems, but at least it's a step in the right direction.

The most rewarding jobs for the young corps members were the ones where they could see a lasting change in what they had done, such as planting trees or working with raptors. During those years that I was leading corps groups, ECC had continued taking in injured raptors. We would rehabilitate them as much as possible and then use them to teach people—mostly children—about wildlife, conservation, and birds of prey. I loved getting up close and working with the raptors, examining their sharp beaks and the different colors of their feathers. Before long I was able to tell a red-tailed hawk from a Cooper's hawk from a Harris's hawk.

One day we got a call from a nonprofit nature sanctuary in Leesburg, Virginia. They had an injured red-tailed hawk that was young and healthy, but would never be able to fly again. That sounded like the type of raptor we might be able to train and use in school presentations. I drove to Leesburg and picked up the bird, which they had named Sky.

When I got back to ECC, I set up Sky in a large cage. She let me examine her wing, which, even though it was permanently damaged, didn't seem to be causing her any pain. Red-tailed hawks are large and fairly common in North America. They are brown, and when they reach adulthood, the feathers on their tails turn some shade of bright brick red. They are one of my favorite species of raptors because they spend much of their time soaring through the air. To me, they are the definition of freedom. Except for Sky.

I fitted an anklet and a jess on her. Red-tailed hawks are also one of the most easily trainable raptors.

"Don't worry that you can't fly, girl," I said to her. "I'll make sure you get plenty of activity."

I started to work with Sky to get to know her personality and her likes and dislikes, in order to determine how she would act during presentations. She seemed to like the attention, and sometimes I would take her out to different parts of Southeast DC to get her used to being around people.

One warm autumn Saturday, I put a handful of dead mice in my leather satchel, wrangled Sky into a crate and headed to Oxon Run Park on Mississippi Avenue SE. Because of the nice weather, lots of kids were running around on the playground, and adults were walking or running on the trails. I put the carrier on a picnic table, slipped my hand into the glove, and pulled Sky out.

It's not every day that people see a tall Black man carrying a large bird, so almost immediately people walked over. I turned my wrist a certain way that prompted Sky to spread her wings. Even with an injury, her four-foot wingspan was impressive, and the small audience clapped.

People started asking me the usual questions, such as "How old is she?," "What does she eat?," and "Where does she live?" Then I made the number-one mistake that anyone working with birds can never, ever make: I stopped paying attention.

Sky was sitting on my glove, and I had already fed her one mouse from my satchel that was hanging on my shoulder. She was still hungry. I was explaining how red-tailed hawks hunt, gesturing with my ungloved hand. I moved my hand too close to Sky, who thought I had food. She jumped from the glove to my bare hand and dug one of her talons into my flesh. *Footing* is the term used when hawks or other raptors grab their prey with their talons, and here Sky was footing me.

Her dagger-sharp talon tore deep into my hand, piercing skin and cartilage. My entire hand felt like it was being crushed with a sledgehammer. Blood spurted out, and I could barely hear the cries of the people around me because the pain was shrouding my entire being. My first instinct was to pull my hand away, but by this time, I had learned enough about raptors to know not to move and not to pull away. That would only cause Sky to dig in deeper, possibly crushing my bones. I tilted and shook my shoulder in a way that upended the satchel of dead mice. A couple of them fell out onto the ground. Sky let go of my hand and jumped to the ground to eat the mice.

I grabbed a towel that was inside Sky's carrier and

wrapped it around my bleeding hand. Sweat was running down my forehead and into my eyes.

"Oh my God," said the woman I had been talking to. "Didn't that hurt? You're acting like it didn't hurt."

"Oh, ma'am, it hurts like hell, pardon my language," I said. "But if I had pulled away, she quite likely would have permanently mangled my hand."

I told the group I had to go, urged Sky back onto my glove and then into the carrier, and headed back to ECC. Once there, I washed my wound with hydrogen peroxide and found a bandage in the First Aid cabinet. I knew that a buddy of mine had some leftover penicillin, so I drove to his house, still feeling a little lightheaded, and he gave me the antibiotics. I didn't want to go to the hospital unless it was absolutely necessary, because I was afraid they might insist that we euthanize Sky. I swallowed a couple of pills, drove home with Sky, and immediately fell asleep.

My hand throbbed for several days but never became infected. The incident with Sky didn't turn me off from working with falcons; it just made me respect these magnificent birds even more. They are hunters, they are food-focused, and Sky couldn't care less about my hand. I had to respect that kind of strength and power.

In 2009, not long after Sky footed me, Bob Nixon started a nonprofit called Wings Over America, located in a one-hundred-year-old farmhouse on more than eight hundred acres in Laurel, Maryland, about a twenty-minute drive from ECC. Also located on the property was the New Beginnings Youth Development Center, a residential program for young men who had committed serious offenses. In a partnership with ECC and the DC Department of Youth Rehabilitation Services, Wings Over America would give the New Beginnings youth a chance to interact with and care for raptors, learn about birds of prey and conservation, and expand on the ECC mission to give young people the tools they need to change their lives and be part of a solution to environmental problems. The idea was that the farmhouse and a few of the other buildings would be restored and turned into a visitor center with aviaries to house raptors and space for educational programming. I was tasked with managing the property and working on the restoration. Ultimately, I would be expanding the raptor work I was already doing at ECC.

As much as I loved working with the raptors and giving presentations with them to young people at risk, I also wanted to work with large birds that weren't injured. I wanted to work with birds that could fly and hunt, and I started to think about falconry. Bob Nixon was a falconer and so was one of the raptor veterinarians we used at ECC. I started researching what falconry was all about, its ancient history, and how falconers hunt their birds, and knew it was something I wanted to do.

Bob gave me his copy of the *California Hawking Club Apprenticeship Manual* and told me the first thing I had to do was find a sponsor. Bob couldn't be my sponsor because he wasn't a licensed falconer in DC or Maryland.

I learned that the sponsor is a critical element to someone becoming a falconer. The sponsor is the person who teaches the ethics, morality, and conservation aspects of trapping and caring for raptors. Close to 75 percent of wild hawks and falcons die before they become adults. Sponsors teach would-be falconers how to identify and trap immature birds, care for them, and eventually release them back into the wild to increase the population. The sponsor makes sure the new falconer is dedicated, knowledgeable, and in it for the long haul. They answer questions and guide new falconers along the path to success. The sponsor agrees to be as available as possible over the two years it takes to reach the next level (general). The apprentice, in turn, must communicate regularly with the sponsor.

Most falconry clubs in the United States, including the North American Falconers Association, have codes of ethics. They can vary from state to state, but all include the basics:

Follow all falconry laws and report those who don't.

Do not keep raptors unless you fly them free during the hunting season.

Keep birds, mews, and equipment in top condition.

Do everything possible to recover a lost bird and to bring a sick raptor back to health.

The sponsor–apprentice relationship is important, and both roles require dedication and patience. I started visiting and calling falconers in Maryland and Virginia. All of them were White and they all seemed surprised that a Black man wanted to be a falconer. One particularly annoying man said to me, "You people don't hunt and fly birds, you eat them."

That old familiar anger began to rise up inside me, but I turned around and walked away from him. When someone tells me I can't do something, it makes me more determined than ever to do it.

If I couldn't find a sponsor, though, my quest to become a falconer would be stuck like a tire in the Anacostia. A few months later, I had stopped by ECC to check on Sky and Mr. Hoots, when Suzanne Shoemaker walked in. She is the director of the Owl Moon Raptor Center in Maryland, a federally and state-licensed rehabilitation center that rescues and rehabs injured, sick, and orphaned birds of prey and returns them to the wild. Suzanne is a licensed master wildlife rehabilitator and would sometimes come to ECC to help us diagnose or administer medicine to a sick raptor.

Suzanne knew more about raptors than just about anyone. The sanctuary she runs is located in several rooms in the basement of her house. That's where her "patients"—owls, hawks, falcons, eagles, and other raptors—are treated and given a chance to recover.

"Hey, Miss Shoemaker," I called when she walked in. "How are you?"

"Hey there, Rodney," she said, giving me a hug. "Long time no see. What's going on?"

Suzanne is also a licensed falconer, so I knew she would understand my falconry dilemma. I told her about how the falconers I had approached said they didn't want to sponsor me and about the idiot who made the racist comment that "you people eat birds."

"Well, gee, Rodney," she said in her laid back manner. "If you want to be a falconer, I'll be your sponsor."

I wasn't expecting that. "You will?"

"Of course I will," Suzanne said. "You already know so much about birds and raptors that I'm sure passing the test will be a breeze for you."

This was great news. It meant my quest to become a falconer was no longer stalled.

A couple of weeks later, I went to Suzanne's sanctuary and we reviewed the *California Hawking Club Apprentice Study Guide* and the *Falconry Manual*. She was right—I already knew much of what was in those books from the hands-on work and presentations I had already been doing at ECC.

After that, things moved faster than I had expected. I spent a few weeks studying and then scheduled the test.

I passed it on my first try and called Suzanne to tell her the news.

"That's great, Rodney," she said. "But I'm not at all surprised."

I laughed.

"You are now a licensed apprentice," she said. "You know what comes next, right?"

"Sure do," I said. "Gotta build my own aviary and then I'm off to trap my first bird. Do you think I can build the aviary in my backyard?" I was living in a town-house in Fort Washington, Maryland, just south of DC.

"Yes, of course," she said. "As long as it's okay with your landlord. In fact, you should be close to your avi-ary because if bad weather hits, you want to still be able to get to them and feed the birds."

My landlord was fine with me building an aviary, so I started collecting two-by-four pieces of wood wherever I could find them. Suzanne gave me a few that she had, and if I was driving and saw some wood by the side of the road, I'd pull over, jump out, and throw it in the car. Eventually I collected enough wood to start build-ing the aviary. My buddy Unk came over to help, and we finished in about a week. Unk was also at my house when the Fish and Wildlife official came to inspect the aviary. It might not have been the prettiest aviary ever, what with so much used wood, but it passed inspection on the first try. That was good enough for me.

Next up: trap a bird to live in my aviary. For the next several months I spent whatever free time I had driving all over the rural areas of Maryland and Virginia, looking for a bird to trap. By mid-January of 2012, I was starting to feel discouraged, but I'm not one to give up so I kept on driving around in my reliable old Mercury Sable, with fresh dead mice or rats in my satchel and my homemade falconer's trap in the trunk.

One cold but sunny day I decided to drive down to Southern Maryland. I hadn't gone there in a while and thought maybe the brisk air would bring out some hungry raptors. St. Mary's County—the southernmost tip of the region—is primarily surrounded by water: the Patuxent River, the Chesapeake Bay, the Potomac River, and the Wicomico River. It also has lots of trees and brush, which means good hunting for raptors.

I was driving slowly down a rural stretch of Leonardtown Road, looking for any hawks or falcons on the prowl, scanning the bare tree limbs, when I saw a large bird land on a branch of a tree about an eighth of a mile from the road. I pulled my car over and jumped out to get a better look. It was a juvenile red-tailed hawk—just what I was hoping for, and my heart started to pound.

Trying to be as quiet and nonthreatening as possible, I set up the trap with a dead rat about five yards from the hawk and then squatted behind some nearby bushes to wait. I had taken my time making the trap after examining Suzanne's traps, reading the manual, and watching some videos online. But would it work? I didn't know.

The hawk seemed interested in the rat but was still sitting on the branch.

"C'mon, now, easy does it," I whispered to no one.

All of a sudden, in the time it took me to blink, the hawk dove onto the rat and was immediately caught in my bal-chatri trap. It worked. My first bird. I was proud, inspired, and a little emotional.

"No time for tears, man," I said to myself. "Let's save that for when we get him safely back to the house.

Because the hawk was smaller than most female red-tails, I knew it was a male. The females are always larger. I approached and held a towel over him with one hand, pressing his body against my thigh, and disentangled his talons from the small nooses of the trap with the other hand. I put him in the nearby carrier and started to laugh. Peering into the carrier, I said, "Well, sir, you are my first bird, and I will care for you until it's time to set you free."

Once a bird has been trapped, falconers usually keep it through one or two winter hunting seasons before releasing it back to the wild as an adult that can hunt on its own.

On the drive home, I decided I would name my first bird Tink, after my buddy from the original ECC group who had been shot and killed. I pulled up in front of my house and carried Tink inside and down to the basement, where my scale and logbook were set up. I weighed him and checked his feathers to make sure no burs were stuck on him, and then I put him in his temporary home: my aviary.

Once Tink was fed and settled, I couldn't wait to tell people that I caught my first raptor. I called Bob Nixon, my old friend Agnes Nixon, Suzanne, Unk, and my kids, and e-mailed photos of Tink to ECC members.

For the next two months I worked with Tink almost every day, training him to fly to my glove when I called and blew the whistle. Red-tailed hawks are known for being relatively easy to train, but I was surprised how quickly Tink learned to fly to the glove. It was soon time to free-fly him outside before setting him free.

Not far from my house was a clearing with woods nearby, and that's where I took my red-tailed hawk to train. One chilly March afternoon, I carried Tink on my glove to the clearing. Just as I lifted my arm so he could take off, a strong gust of wind came along and carried Tink upward. He was forced to fly to a tree that was farther away than the one we usually used, but when he landed, a murder of big, fat crows started flapping around him and screeching. Tink had no choice but to take off.

I spent the rest of the afternoon blowing the whistle and running through the woods looking for him, but he was gone. The sun was setting so I went home, sat in my dark living room, and cried. I knew that I was going to release Tink anyway, but my plan had been to have a little ceremony when I did it, in honor of Tink the man, and then set Tink the raptor free. Nature had other plans. It was an important lesson to learn.

For the next few months I continued working on constructing the aviaries at Wings Over America in Laurel and trapping birds to live in my own aviary at my house.

Once we began to bring some of the raptors from ECC to Wings Over America, Bob said they would have to arrange for someone to live on the property because live animals were going to be there. I was already running ECC's raptor program and I had my own birds now, so it made sense for me to be the onsite manager. That way, ECC wouldn't have to create a new position and I could save a little money by living rent-free. A large trailer was placed on-site at the Laurel location, with the idea that we would eventually rehab one of the old buildings on the property into a house. In the meantime, the trailer suited all of my needs and—best of all—I would be living near woods, nature, and open space.

At the end of March, when the trailer was ready for me to move in, I transported my belongings and the two birds I had recently trapped to Laurel, my new home. The next day I'd be bringing Sky and Mr. Hoots from ECC to Laurel, and then I could really start to get Wings Over America up and running.

The first night I spent in the trailer at Laurel was surprisingly warm for March, and the fresh smells of coming spring lingered on the breeze. I opened the trailer door, lay down on the bed, and listened to the sounds of nature at night. I thought about the past ten years of my life and how many changes I have been through. If someone had told twenty-one-year-old me that not only would I be alive at age forty-one but I would be managing a raptor program, on my way to becoming a master falconer, teaching young people, caring about the planet, bonding with nature on so many levels, and—most of all—doing things that I loved, I would have laughed my ass off.

Somehow, though, each thing—good and bad—that had happened to me in life so far seemed like a puzzle piece that fit perfectly with another piece, and that fit with another piece, and so on. It was meant to all fit together. I didn't know what the puzzle would look like when it was finished, but I was ready for whatever life might bring.

These were the thoughts I had as I drifted off to sleep that first night in my trailer.

Chapter 11

"You can do this," I say. "You already got the glove on. You're halfway there."

I'm holding Mr. Hoots, the large Eurasian eagle-owl, about four feet away from a ten-year-old girl. She is part of a class trip that is here to visit Rodney's Raptors and learn about what I do.

Rodney's Raptors is the nonprofit I started when Wings Over America began to get requests for demonstrations at birthday parties and individual falconry lessons, which isn't the mission of Wings Over America, whose primary audience is at-risk teenagers. Now I manage both programs.

We're in the presentation room at the Laurel property, and about twenty middle school students are sitting on metal chairs watching what's going to happen.

"What's your name?"

"Shondra."

"Look, Shondra, I promise you that this bird won't hurt you," I say. "I know he's big and scary-looking, but he is friendly."

Some of her classmates call out, "You got this, Shonny."

Shondra looks at Mr. Hoots, who stares back at her with his pumpkin-colored eyes. She looks at me, then back at Hoots. I try to remember if I was afraid of Mr. Hoots the first time I held him all those years ago. Probably, although I'm sure I wouldn't have admitted it. He and I are bonded for life now.

"Hold your arm out," I say.

Shondra nervously stretches out a skinny arm encased in one of my leather gloves. "Now turn your hand a little so your thumb is facing up. Good, good."

Mr. Hoots is sitting on my gloved hand, and I move closer so he can jump to her glove. I hear Shondra take a breath as he lands, just inches from her face. Everyone is quiet for a few seconds, and then Shondra's classmates start cheering.

"Keep your arm up, keep your arm up," I shout.

Shondra holds her arm up and starts to laugh. "I—I did it," she says.

"Of course you did," I say.

She laughs again, and I let Mr. Hoots jump back to

my glove. He spreads his wings wide—all six feet of them—and the children ooh and ahh.

Shondra sits back down with her classmates, who are patting her on the back and giving her high fives. She is clearly proud of herself. And this is what I love. Now it's time for my little lecture on fear.

Mr. Hoots is still sitting on my glove, and I pick up a dead white mouse to feed him as a reward. He grabs it with his beak.

The kids start to shout, "*Eww!* That's so gross."

"What?" I ask, pretending to be serious. "You want to try one? I heard they taste like chicken."

"No! No way!" they scream, and we all start laughing.

"Okay, seriously, now," I say. "What did Shondra just do?"

One boy raises his hand. "She held that hawk."

"This isn't a hawk. I'll show you a hawk in a few minutes and we'll see who wants to hold that. Who remembers what kind of bird this is?"

"An owl," calls out another boy.

"That's right," I say. "So, yes, Shondra held an owl. Most people never hold an owl in their entire lives. But she did something way, way bigger than that. You were scared at first, right?"

Shondra nods her head. I continue.

"She was afraid, but she let this large bird with sharp talons sit on her hand. She just did one of the biggest things she will ever do in her life: She overcame her fear. Think about something that scares you. Okay now, if you can learn how to not be afraid of that, then you'll be able to do anything you want. I'll tell you a little secret about how this works: the next time Shondra is afraid of something or thinking she can't do something, she will remember this day and say to herself, 'Well, if I could overcome my fear and hold that huge scary owl, then I can overcome my fear now and do this thing.' Sometimes you just have to get out of your own damn way."

The kids start to giggle.

"Oops," I say, holding my hand up to mouth. "I mean, sometimes you have to get out of your own DARN way. *Darn.*"

The two teachers standing in the back smile and shake their heads.

A boy who has been sitting quietly in the back row raises his hand and says, "Can I try it?"

"Holding the owl?" I say. He nods his head.

"Sure, come on up here. Are you a little afraid?" He nods his head again.

I go through the process with him just like I did with Shondra. When Hoots jumps from my glove to his, the little boy laughs out loud, revealing where he recently lost a front tooth.

"See that," I say. "I am so proud of you. You were scared and you did it anyway."

The presentation ends, and the teachers start lining up the students to return to their vehicles. I notice that the little boy with the missing tooth is standing at the back of the line and that he is crying quietly.

I walk over and stoop down next to him. "Hey little man-man," I say. "What's the matter? You just did something amazing."

He wipes his eyes with the back of his hand and looks at me like he's not sure if he can trust me. I lean my head down so he can whisper in my ear. In a low voice he says, "Nobody ever said they were proud of me before."

"Aw, shoot," I say, giving him a high five. "I'm saying it to you now. I. Am. Proud. Of. You. Got it? And don't ever forget it."

He nods and smiles and runs to catch up with his classmates.

I love working with kids like this from inner-city schools. I know what they're going through. Some of them have parents who are gang-banging, or drug addicts, or abusive. My own father wasn't around much. Basically, the two things he ever did for me was buy me a Popsicle and beat me. He was murdered when I was fifteen. I know what it's like to be poor, to be hungry, to slice through one of those blocks of bright yellow government cheese—although I think the food stamp system has changed now. But I also remember the hopelessness, and the feeling that I would never get out of the projects. My goal with these younger kids is to help them understand that there's a way. There is always a way.

I switch up my presentations depending on what age group I'm talking with. I talk to the younger kids about getting past their fears. As I've tried to teach my own children, fear can be a crutch that people lean on their whole lives. Pretty soon, almost everything becomes a crutch, and what have you done in your life? I want these kids to throw away their crutches and understand that they have choices.

To the older middle and high school kids and the young people from Capital Guardian Youth Challenge Academy, I'm more frank about my story. The drugs, the guns, jail. I don't glamorize the hustling, and I downplay the money aspect. My message to them is that if I didn't get into animals and the environment, I'd have either died in the streets or been locked up for life. And what are they going to get into so that they don't die in the streets? It can get a little raw sometimes. I tell them how when someone is murdered, it's not just that one person, but that the sadness moves out like a tsunami, crushing mothers, brothers, sisters, friends, entire families. I tell them about Monique. Some people think that because we're poor and Black and have seen a lot of death, that we're immune to it. You never get immune to murder. That's why, ever since Monique was killed, I've had insomnia and can't sleep more than three or four hours at a time.

It can be frustrating sometimes, and I think maybe my work doesn't make a difference, because the problems of Southeast DC are so entrenched. But other days, I think that if I can motivate even just one kid to put down his gun and look for something else, then maybe I have succeeded.

Since I've been running Wings Over America and Rodney's Raptors, the number of presentations and talks I'm invited to give is increasing. People seem naturally drawn to the awe-inspiring beauty and power of raptors. No matter their background, age, or culture, people are fascinated by the big birds. For example, every year I'm invited to bring my birds to the Annual Monacan Nation Powwow held in Elon, Virginia. Members of the Monacan Nation have inhabited parts of Virginia, particularly in Amherst County, for more than 10,000 years. They understand the majesty of raptors, and always ask me to return. I take my birds to block parties, events at the Anacostia Watershed, and even parties for the Washington Nationals, DC's Major League Baseball team.

For the past few years I've been giving demonstrations at the Patuxent Research Refuge, located on more than twelve thousand acres of land situated between

Baltimore and Washington, DC. Established more than eighty years ago, the refuge surrounds the Patuxent and Little Patuxent Rivers and is pulsing with wildlife, from miniscule insects to deer and eagles. Its mission is to conserve and protect the natural habitats through research, teaching, and wildlife management techniques.

The refuge is home to more than sixty species of water- and shorebirds, more than one hundred species of land birds, almost countless mammals from the little brown bat to the long-tailed weasel, and all kinds of amphibians, fish, reptiles, butterflies, and assorted insects. And of course, numerous native plants and trees. It's like this huge outdoor research laboratory.

When I wander the grounds of the refuge, I feel like I am in my own natural habitat. I breathe the clean air and let the sights and sounds nourish my soul. Sometimes, I inhale deeply and in that small space right before the exhale, I imagine part of this wildlife air stays inside of me, circulating in my blood.

The day before, I had showed Mr. Hoots to Shondra and her classmates, and today I'm on my way to Patuxent. One of the missions of the refuge center is to educate people young and old and help them engage directly with wildlife. That's where I come in. Patuxent is holding a Visitor's Day, where staff members and researchers give demonstrations and point out wildlife habitats. Mr. Hoots and Agnes are in carriers in the back of my van. They are my best-behaved raptors, so I often use them to teach.

I enter the property off Powder Mill Road and drive down the winding, one-lane road toward the visitor's center. The parking guard sees me approaching and waves.

"Birdman, how are you?"

"Good, I'm good," I say. Lots of people at Patuxent and other places call me "the birdman"; some don't even know my real name.

I grab the carriers and my glove and head around behind the building, where it's a little quieter, and the birds won't get nervous. It's a sunny October day, and unusually warm—the kind of autumn day that has the last taste of summer on its lips. It feels good, but I'm also looking forward to the colder days when I can hunt my birds.

I keep Agnes in her carrier and put her in a room in the visitor center. I don my glove and take Mr. Hoots out of his carrier. We sit out in the sun on a low wall that surrounds a patio. From here I look out over the Patuxent River and watch a flock of low-flying Canada geese, honking to one another, which always sounds sad to me. Canada geese mate for life. Whenever I see them flying over in their V-formation, I count how many are there. If it's an even number, chances are they are all with their mates. An odd number means someone's flying solo, like me.

I'm scheduled to be here at the refuge for three hours, giving twenty-minute presentations with ten-minute breaks in between.

One of the refuge volunteer guides comes around the corner with the first group, made up of about a dozen Asian American children and adults. I don't know if they are all one family or friends, but it doesn't matter. They want to be here. And, like clockwork, when the kids see Mr. Hoots they start pointing and jumping up and down.

They sit in a semi-circle around me, and the guide introduces me. The children look to be between the ages of six and ten. I introduce them to Mr. Hoots.

"How old is he?" one child calls out.

"Mr. Hoots here is twenty-six," I say, moving my arm up and down a little, which prompts the owl to spread his wings. "He's what we call a Eurasian eagle-owl, and he's waving to you. In the wild, this kind of owl can survive up to about thirty years, but in captivity they live longer. The oldest one in captivity that I've heard about lived sixty-five years."

"Why is his name Mr. Hoots?" asks another.

"Because that's what he does all night long," I say, making a hooting sound. Then Mr. Hoots replies, and the children laugh. "If he lived with you, you'd have to put cotton in your ears every night because his hooting would keep you awake."

One shy little girl raises her hand.

"Yes, baby girl," I say. "What's your question?"

She stands up and points to Mr. Hoots. "Um, what does he eat?"

"That's a great question," I say. "Mostly, Mr. Hoots eats mice or maybe snakes. If he came to live with you, that's what you would have to feed him. You couldn't just make him a peanut butter and jelly sandwich, you know."

The twenty minutes pass by quickly, and the guide returns with another group of about four small families, two who are African American and two who are White. That's one of the amazing things about nature and wildlife: it's always colorblind. It's here for all of us, no matter what color, age, or background. Somewhere along the way, humans started to think that we were better than the animals and the birds, better than the land, and we got high thinking we could control it. Power and control are just as addictive as heroin and cocaine. That led to destruction of habitats and over-developed areas. We have already destroyed so much of this planet. Sometimes I feel like the role I play is too little, that I need to do more, but I haven't figured out yet what more is.

The families settle down, and I run through my demonstration with Mr. Hoots.

"Do you all want to see another bird?" I ask. Of course, the kids cheer and the adults clap. I take Mr. Hoots inside, put him in his carrier and bring out Agnes.

As docile as Agnes is, with her large shoulders and sharp beak, she looks intimidating to those who don't know her.

"Does anyone know what kind of bird this is?" I ask. The children in this group are older than those in the last group.

"A falcon," one boy says.

"That is a great guess," I say, "but Agnes here is a Harris's hawk."

"How do you know that's what she is?"

I turn Agnes around and show them her coppery tail feathers.

"There are other ways to tell, too," I say. "See how her chest is kind of big? That's another way to tell. Most hawks aren't so beefy. And the feathers on their shoulders usually form the shape of a white letter V."

One of the mothers now raises her hand.

"Yes, ma'am," I say.

"So there are different kinds of hawks?"

"Oh yes," I answer. "And they all have different traits and identifying marks. Take the Harris's hawk, for instance. It learns fast and has a great memory—probably better than yours or mine. They have long legs and sometimes, if there aren't a lot of trees around, they'll stand on top of one another to better spot their prey; they work as a group."

I explain how the more they research and look for large raptors, the easier it becomes to tell them apart.

When the day comes to an end I pack up Mr. Hoots and Agnes, put them in the van, and visit for a little while with some of the Patuxent employees. Everyone who works or volunteers at Patuxent wants to be here, just like me. The ebb and flow of nature runs through our blood.

I drive back to Laurel, get Mr. Hoots and Agnes settled, let my dog Munna out, feed the horses, and watch the sun set.

I've been a general falconer for about five years now. In a few short months, I will attain my status as master falconer. The final step in my falconry journey. What is going to come next for me? I've started to feel restless because I'm ready for the next big thing in my life, the next puzzle piece to fall into place. I just don't know what it is yet. I do know what it will include: raptors, animals, wide open spaces, and helping kids. Of course, that's what I'm doing now. Is it possible to do all of that on a more vast and immense level? And what would that even look like? I'm determined to find out.

Chapter 12

2018

Mike is standing on the corner of Valley Avenue SE and Fourth Street SE, holding my Harris's hawk, Agnes. To say he is attracting attention would be an understatement. Mike has adopted my practice of taking a raptor into the city to educate and fascinate.

I stand nearby watching little kids, teenagers, and adults gather around him, curious and smiling. Mike is a general falconer now. As his sponsor, I had to sign papers stating that he had met all of the falconry standards and was worthy of obtaining his general license. He hasn't trapped a raptor since Gorgeous Isabella Flowers died, but Mike has a twenty-year-old Harris's hawk named Old Timer that was given to him by another falconer. But today, instead of flying his own hawk, he wanted to bring Agnes into the city. Mike is the only person I trust to handle Agnes safely. I just came along for the ride.

He is patient with the onlookers as they pepper him with questions.

"What kinda bird is that?"

"It's called a Harris's hawk."

"What do you do with it?"

"I'm a falconer," says Mike, and he looks at me and smiles.

He explains how he hunts the hawks and what they eat. One little boy's eyes get bigger and bigger.

"Do they eat people too?" he says.

Mike laughs. "No, they don't eat people. You don't have to be afraid of Agnes here. You just have to respect her."

To some of the teenagers and adults who wander over, Mike tells them how flying and hunting raptors makes him feel like he's connecting with something bigger and how it gives him a sense of peace after a harrowing day of being a firefighter. Then they start asking him what it's like to be a fireman.

This morning, when we were getting Agnes out of the aviary, Mike said to me, "You know, I got this from you."

"Got what from me?"

"Wanting to show people that there's more to life than just their everyday lives," he said. "Helping people see that there's always something bigger than you in life and that you just have to embrace that. And if you're not sure what that something bigger is, then nature is a great place to start."

Mike and I both hope that when other people of color see us interacting with our birds or horses, it will give them a sense of inspiration that they can explore and experience anything they want.

After about an hour hanging out on Valley Avenue talking to people about raptors, Mike and I decide to pack up.

"Okay, Agnes, you ready to go?" I say. I put my glove on and Mike flies Agnes to me. Some of the kids start clapping. I put Agnes back in her carrier and climb into the driver's seat. I'm giving a presentation at Patuxent this afternoon and Mike has to pick up his kids. But first, I have some major news to share that I've been keeping secret. As we pull into my driveway, I decide to lay it on him.

"Oh, by the way, Goob," I casually say. "Forgot to tell you, I bought a house."

He looks at me and starts laughing. "Man, you trippin'."

"Goober. Listen to me. I. Bought. A. House. It's in Virginia, and I have big plans for it."

I pull out my phone to show Mike pictures of the property.

Last year, as I was thinking about what my next big thing would be, I realized that whatever it is, it wasn't going to happen as long as I was living in a trailer on someone else's property. I needed my own space.

In the spring, when I was giving a raptor demonstration at the Annual Monacan Indian Nation Powwow, I met a Native falconer named Jesse. We started talking about our birds and the sense of peace and freedom we both felt when flying raptors. We walked around the powwow, watching colorful dance and drum competitions and chowing down on Indian tacos, corn soup, and fry bread. I told Jesse about feeling restless and wanting to own property for a change. Turns out Jesse's son was a real estate agent, and I called him a few days after the powwow.

I liked the idea of using an agent who was Monacan. Even though I'm African American, I have always felt a kindred connection with indigenous people. Maybe it grows from the shared history of deep pain and discrimination. Collective trauma doesn't dissolve; it gets passed down from generation to generation, each one interpreting it, trying to escape it. I envision racism like a gigantic weed. Each new generation that comes along tries to create a path by cutting down parts of the weed. But until we, as a nation, acknowledge that the weed exists, that it's there, and that it is choking other plants, preventing them from growing and sometimes even killing them; until we all start digging and digging and pull that weed out by its giant roots, then it's not going anywhere.

I decided to look at properties in rural Virginia, because I have family there and also in DC. The first five houses I saw didn't impress me. Either they were too close to people or too expensive. The agent told me about a house in small Charlotte Courthouse, Virginia, about a four-hour drive from Laurel. When I arrived, I saw a one-level brick house, nothing out of the ordinary. It was nice enough, with three bedrooms and updated amenities. What struck me, though, was the surrounding property. The modest house sat on seven acres of wooded land. I went out the back door and started walking around the grounds, into the woods. The pulse of wildlife was present. I looked up and saw a red-tailed hawk at the top of an oak tree, and I started to laugh. Surely this was a sign. I walked back to the house, sat on the back deck, and closed my eyes.

The sense of my mom's spirit surrounded me, and I hadn't felt that at the other houses I had looked at. Clear as if she was standing next to me, I heard her voice say, "This is it."

When I opened my eyes, I no longer saw trees and grass, I saw Dippy's Dream—a sanctuary for raptors and animals, a campground for underprivileged kids, a stable with horses, a petting zoo, a baseball field, vegetable gardens, a conservation hut, and nature trails. This was the missing puzzle piece. I would create a place where animals and raptors could live safely and where kids from Southeast DC and other cities could come and learn how to grow food, ride horses, interact with birds and animals, identify plants, and be safe, at least for a week or so.

"I hear you, Dippy," I said and laughed again. When the real estate agent pulled into the driveway, I walked to his car and said, "I'll take it."

He looked surprised. "But, don't you want to . . ."

"I said, I'll take it."

And that was that.

Until now, the only other person I have told is Unk. He said I could count on him to help draw up the plans for Dippy's Dream.

I don't tell Mike all of my ideas for the new property yet, because I'm still working them out in my head.

"Dad, I can't believe you bought a house, and you're just telling me now," he says.

"I know, but soon enough I'll share my plans with you. I'm still figuring it all out."

Mike hugs me and gets in his car to leave. As he's about to pull out he calls out the window, "Oh hey, Dad, I know why you bought that house."

"You do?"

"Yeah, *I* bought a house, so now *you* had to go buy a

house. Looks like I'm in the lead," he says laughing and pulls out of the driveway.

Our lifelong friendly competition is alive and well. Last week he told me his goal was to become a stronger falconer than I am. Talk about somebody trippin'— shoot, *I* am the master falconer. I did it first, and that will never change. Mike has to come up with something better than that—and I have no doubt that he will.

I watch Mike drive off. Things are going well, and I have finally achieved some major goals that I set for myself. I'm in a good position to pursue Dippy's Dream.

A few days after I told Mike about my new house, I call my brother Chuck to let him know.

"Congratulations, bro," Chuck says. For our entire lives, Chuck has always been in my corner. "When do I get to see it?"

"Soon, soon," I say. I tell him about all of the land and how I'm going to have to clear some of it to make room for the stable, aviary, and other parts of the sanctuary.

Chuck says he's going to stop by and see me at Laurel later this week. I haven't seen him in about three months. We talk on the phone several times a week, but I've been busy with raptor demonstrations, and I haven't had time to go see him.

A few days later, Chuck pulls into my driveway and gets out of his car. He has always been stocky, but the person who gets out of the car is thin. Almost bony.

"Hey, Fat Man," I call out, using one of Chuck's longtime nicknames. The other one is Big Chuck. "You're not fat. What's going on? You on crack or something?" I joke.

Chuck laughs. "No, bro, I'm just getting into shape. You know, none of us is getting any younger. Hey, I got you a present."

He walks around to the trunk of his car and pulls out a weed whacker. "To help get your new place in shape," he says.

As Chuck walks toward me carrying the weed whacker, I notice he is limping. "What, you hurt your leg with all that getting-into-shape foolishness?" I ask.

Chuck tells me that he has had a cut on his foot for several weeks and that it isn't getting any better.

"I think it might be infected, Slim," he says.

"Look man, I know you hate hospitals and all that—so do I—but you have to call the doctor," I say. "Look, if Dippy was here, she would drag your ass to the doctor herself."

We both laugh at the thought of Dippy pushing Chuck out the door to see the doctor.

I am touched that Chuck brought me a housewarming present, and the weed whacker will certainly help.

I ask Chuck if he wants to drive to Virginia now to see the property, but he says he's not up for it. He looks tired.

We sit on a low wall near my trailer and talk. I tell Chuck all about my plans for Dippy's Dream. He's almost more excited about it than I am. Chuck and I have always encouraged each other's ideas. He was one of the few people who didn't think I was crazy when I said I wanted to become a falconer. I also tell him about Mike becoming a general falconer.

We reminisce about some of our younger, crazier days, and the trouble we used to run up against while hustling drugs and hanging out on the streets.

"Man, I'm glad we both made it out alive," Chuck says, patting me on the back. "I used to wonder sometimes if we would."

Several days after Chuck gave me the weed whacker, he finally relents and goes to the doctor, and the news isn't good. Chuck has diabetes, and the doctor admits him to the hospital. They have to amputate all of the toes on his right foot.

I call Chuck the day after the surgery, and he sounds pretty good. Our sister Shanell is with him, and I try to stay upbeat even though I have no idea how he's going to get around without toes. Can someone walk without toes? I have no idea.

"Look, Fat Man," I say. "Think of all the crap we've been through. This is gonna be easy for you. I'll help you recover, because you have to help me build Dippy's Dream. I can't do it without you."

Chuck says he has to go because the doctor just came in to check on him.

"I'll call you back later, Rodney," he says.

"All right, man," I say. "I love you."

"Love you too, bruh," says Chuck.

The next morning, I'm at my Virginia property, and I'm a little pissed because Chuck hasn't called me back like he promised. When my phone finally rings, I am ready to cuss him out, but Shanell is on the other line, and she is crying.

"Rodney, Chuck is gone," she sobs. "He's dead, Rodney."

"Hold up, hold up!" I shout. "What the hell are you talking about?"

Shanell explains that when the doctor came to the room yesterday, he said that removing Chuck's toes wasn't enough and that they were going to have to amputate his entire foot.

"Rodney, the minute the doctor said they have to cut off his foot, Chuck's whole manner changed," says Shanell. "It was like the air went out of him and he said, 'Man, I'm just so tired.'"

I run to my car while still talking to Shanelle so I can get back to DC. She explains that this morning they wanted to move Chuck to a different hospital room but when he tried to get out of bed, he collapsed.

"Oh, Rodney," says Shanell in between sobs, "it was so awful. He flat-lined right there in the room. They were able to get his heart beating, but then it stopped again, and this time they couldn't bring him back. I can't believe this is happening. How can Chuck be dead?" Now she was crying uncontrollably, and I tell her I'll meet her at the hospital.

By the time I get there, Mike, Little Rodney, and some other family members have gathered. I hug Shanell. She looks exhausted. Chuck's doctor tells us that it wasn't the diabetes that killed Chuck but a pulmonary embolism.

We walk out of the hospital in silence, hugging one another and crying. This isn't supposed to happen. Chuck is only forty-nine.

I return to Laurel and feed my birds and horses. I decide to ride my horse Bailey around the property for a little while to clear my head. I knew Chuck had a pulmonary embolism, but I have other thoughts about what happened.

Chuck had lived with our mom for almost his entire life. After she died, he continued living in her apartment. They were close, and Dippy's death hit Chuck even harder than it did me. I think that the first time Chuck flat-lined, he saw Mom smiling at him and telling him how proud she was of him. Then the doctors brought him back to life, but he didn't want to come back. He wanted to be with Mom. He missed our mother that much.

Now both of my rocks are gone, and I feel adrift, like a piece of trash floating in the old Anacostia. If I don't have a steady foundation to walk on, how will I keep going?

What a twisted hell of a ride this has been. My soul feels abused, and even the rhythm of my heartbeat has changed.

I think about canceling a couple of raptor demonstrations I'm supposed to give this week because I don't know if I'm ever going to stop crying. Then I remember how my mom used to tell us that self-pity was the worst thing you can have. I can hear her say, "Okay, you can have five minutes to feel sorry for yourself. That's 300 seconds. Clock is ticking, you'd better get started."

My five minutes are up. Somehow I have to find the light inside of my darkness. I'm convinced that the secret lies in the creation of Dippy's Dream. It's going to be a heavy lift for me, especially without Chuck around to encourage me when things get rough. But I have Unk and my kids and grandkids, and they believe in me.

Later this week, I'm going to look for machinery to rent so I can start clearing some of the trees in Virginia. And tonight I am going back to the drawing board—literally, a table set up in the demonstration room—to work on the renderings for Dippy's Dream. I'm moving forward. I hear Agnes squawk from inside her aviary.

"That's right, Agnes," I call, as I climb off Bailey and lead him back to his space. "We're doing it."

Chapter 13

2018

My neck is stiff from leaning over the table. I'm working on the blueprint for Dippy's Dream, but I need to take a break and clear my head.

"C'mon, Munna," I say to my white pit bull, who's been lying at my feet, patiently waiting for attention.

She jumps up and starts galloping in circles, tail wagging.

"Lord, you're a silly one. C'mon, let's roll."

She trots next to me as I walk around the property, checking on the aviaries and making sure the horses are okay. All four of them—Bailey, Ninja, Dippy, and Gnip—come galloping across the field to me when I call and whistle. It's a chilly December afternoon, and the horses snort steam out of their nostrils like little smokestacks.

I spent all day yesterday at the house in Virginia, taking measurements of the land, figuring out what was going to go where, and researching types of materials and machinery I'm going to need to turn seven acres in Virginia into Dippy's Dream. Once I move to Virginia full time, I know I will miss seeing the Anacostia River on a regular basis. That river and I have grown up together, come of age together. From playing on its banks as a child to cleaning the crap outs of its very bowels, I feel like the river runs through me as naturally as my own blood. But the new life the river gave me is exactly what I hope to share with visitors to Dippy's Dream. I'll still come back to DC to give presentations and of course visit my kids and Unk, but it will feel strange not having the Anacostia so close.

Munna and I go back inside, literally back to the drawing board. I'm using the measurements I took yesterday to plan what will go where. I run my finger over the work I've already done. The house is about fifty yards from the road and is surrounded by a huge half-circle mass of trees on the sides and around the back. To the right of the house is where the vegetable garden will be. I want to be able to grow as much food as possible and teach others how to grow their own food. Further down from the garden will be enclosures for the goats and chickens and maybe a petting zoo as well. Directly behind the house is where I'll build the aviary. Old horse stables already exist on the property, and I just need to fix them up a bit. Farther away from the house is where I'll clear some trees and grow grass for the campground, with room for about three small cabins and several tents. What have I forgotten? We'll need some type of pantry/kitchen area where food can be stored and prepared; maybe that could be set up on the first floor of my house. There's still so much to figure out. The first step will be to clear a bunch of trees and underbrush. How will I be able to afford the equipment I need to do that?

For a minute, I start to feel overwhelmed. This is the biggest thing I've ever taken on in my life. The Virginia house needs a new roof. And I have to buy a tractor to start clearing the land, and they can cost well over twenty-five thousand dollars. How will I do it?

I rub my hands over my face. I have to stay focused on why I'm doing this. The prize is that Dippy's Dream will be a place where kids from the inner city, at-risk youth, and other young people can have a respite from violence and poverty. A place where they don't have to grow up so fast, where they can learn self-confidence and self-sufficiency. A place where they can be curious and experience wonder. And most importantly, a place where they can be a part of something bigger than they are: nature, sky, earth, trees, birds, animals. Dippy's Dream will be free for those who cannot afford to pay. My philosophy is that just because someone is poor doesn't mean they don't deserve to have a positive, uplifting experience. Of course, this philosophy means I will have to step up my fundraising efforts.

In addition to planning the details of Dippy's Dream, I'm still giving regular presentations for Rodney's Raptors and ECC's Wings Over America. Thanks to some local media attention and word of mouth, I've been busier than ever. In the past couple of years, I've traveled to public schools in Philadelphia, Fairfax, Alexandria, Baltimore, and New Brunswick; summer camps; and city festivals, talking about raptors and conservation.

If an audience of people wants to learn, I go. It doesn't matter how big or small the venue—I've presented at Wild Birds Unlimited nature shops, the National Park Trust, the National Wildlife Federation, and the International Association for Falconry and Conservation of Birds of Prey.

Earlier this year, I gave a talk at the Yale School of Forestry and Environmental Studies. That was the first time I spoke at a university. Dippy would have been proud. I also met with university students during a presentation at the Saudi Young Leaders International Exchange

Program, which aims to promote mutual understanding, civic responsibility, and diversity between young people from Saudi Arabia and the United States.

The liveliest presentations I give are probably the ones at the tailgate parties with the Screaming Eagles, the official fan club of the major league soccer club called DC United. The team plays at Audi Stadium, which is within walking distance of the Matthew Henson Earth Conservation Center--the ECC headquarters. Members of the fan club tailgate on a grassy area near the center, and I bring some of the raptors outside for them to meet and learn about. It's a party atmosphere, with music and food, and the fans are enthusiastic about the upcoming soccer game.

As much as I prefer to be alone with my birds and animals, I have to admit that I thrive on sharing my wonder of nature with others. This past June, however, something happened that meant more to me than the attention I've been getting: I reached the level of master falconer.

Logistically speaking, it doesn't seem like such a big deal. No framed certificate is delivered, no test is passed, no party. Once general falconers have achieved five years of practice, they mail in the fee for their annual license, and when it comes back, it says "Master Falconer" on it instead of "General Falconer."

When the envelope arrived, I knew that was the day. I carefully opened the envelope, and there it was, printed in the right-hand corner of the license: "Rodney Vaughn Stotts, Master Falconer." I laughed out loud. After seven years, I had reached my goal.

I whistled for Munna, and we jumped in my car. I put the license in the glove compartment and started to drive. My destination was Fort Lincoln Cemetery in nearby Prince George's County. That's where my mom is buried, and I wanted to share my news with her.

Like most cemeteries, Fort Lincoln is peaceful and hilly, with lots of manicured grass and trees. I put the license in my pocket and walked right to her gravestone. I brushed away some stray leaves and stared at her name etched in the stone.

"Well, Dippy," I said. "I did it." I pulled the license out of my pocket, unfolded it, and held it up. "You are looking at your son, Rodney Stotts, master falconer." I laughed out loud and fist-bumped the air.

"Ma, you believed in me when nobody else did," I said. "Other people laughed when I told them I wanted to become a master falconer. But not you. I can still see you listening to me, thinking about what I was saying, and nodding your head. And I remember what you said: 'Rodney, if you believe in yourself and if you believe you can do this, then I know you will do it.' And I did it, Ma. I did it."

I stayed at the cemetery for a little while, just breathing in the stillness and the peace of all the souls laid to rest here and thinking about my mom. I heard a bark from the car—Munna telling me it was time to go.

I called my son, Mike, my original sponsor, Suzanne, and a few other people to share my news. A few weeks later, the Screaming Eagles posted a photo of me along with a congratulatory message on their social media platforms.

And now here I am, working toward a new goal that seems bigger than all of the other ones combined. Unlike in my younger years, I have a plan this time around—I just have to figure out how to execute it.

I call Mike on the phone.

"Hey, Goober, what's up? Are you free tomorrow?"

"Hey, Dad, yeah I'm off tomorrow. What's going on?"

"It's supposed to be a calm, chilly day, you know?"

Mike starts laughing. "Oh man, you wanna fly?"

Mike and I haven't flown birds together since last winter. Falconry is a seasonal effort, and winter is the best time to fly and hunt raptors. The rest of the year they are molting and breeding.

I fold up the plans for Dippy's Dream and put them away for now, but I want to show them to Unk soon. He is good at organizing things and thinking through problems. I just need to be patient, trust the process, and try not to get in my own damn way—just like I tell the kids I work with.

I look forward to Mike coming over. Being outside, flying my birds will help me get out of my head for a little while and stay in the present. When I am out-side—especially with a raptor—I feel like I am home. Whether I'm worried, anxious, angry, or trying to fig-ure out a problem—everything falls into place.

Mike arrives in the morning and has his kids, Ayden, Amina, and Journee, with him. They jump out of the car with their usual burst of enthusiasm.

"Pop Pop!" they call out, Ayden and Amina run toward me, and Journee stops to hug Munna.

I give out bear hugs and then pick up Journee and swing her around in a circle.

"You all ready to fly some birds today?" I ask them.

"Yes, yes!" they shout.

I slap Mike on the back and tell him about how the plans for Dippy's Dream are progressing. I also con-fide my concerns about how long it's going to take and whether my finances—or maybe I should say "lack of" finances—will interrupt things.

"Well, Dad," Mike says. "Like you used to tell us, if you can't give it your best shot, then don't bother doing it, and I've never known you to start something and not finish it."

We decide to fly my Harris's hawks, Squeal and Agnes. First up is Agnes. I go into her aviary, attach a jess to her ankle, and clip a creance on her. Then I carry her out and let the kids greet her.

"Her toes look scary," says Amina.

"They're called *talons*, not toes," I say. "And they *are* sharp and scary. That's why you have to wear a glove like this one."

Mike has gone into the other aviary and now has Squeal on his glove. As his name implies, Squeal is squawking his head off.

"What's he saying, Pop Pop?" asks Journee.

"He says, 'I love that little girl named Journee, but I need to fly in the sky, man.'"

Journee giggles. "Can I hold him?"

"Yeah, me too, me too!" cries Ayden.

"You all know you got to be a little bit bigger," says Mike, "but c'mon, you can help me and Pop Pop fly them."

Mike is so kind and patient with his children. Much more patient than I had been with Mike and his siblings. I had been strict with them because I was just so afraid that they would fall prey to the street. It's ironic because I was hustling on the streets with one hand, and trying to keep them away from the streets with the other.

With the birds on our gloves and the kids following behind, we walk away from the road and electrical wires and closer to the woods. Amina is skipping to keep up with us. We stop in a small clearing surrounded by tall, bare trees.

"This looks like a good spot," I say. I unclip the creance attached to Agnes and drop it on the ground. "Okay, let's do this."

On signal, Mike and I lift our gloved arms, and Agnes and Squeal fly up and up. Their wide wings almost seem to move in slow motion. Even though Agnes is a Harris's hawk, she has some reddish feathers on her wings, and they glint in the pale sunlight. For a minute, Squeal and Agnes fly next to each other, partners silhouetted against the winter sky. Agnes starts to fly a little higher, but Squeal catches up and they both land on the high branches of two adjacent trees. We all watch in silence.

"I wish I could fly," says Ayden.

"Me too, little man, me too," I say.

But flying these birds is the next best thing. When I release a bird, watch it fly, and then call it back, I feel peace and clarity and a sense that my heart is lifting.

I blow my whistle first, and Agnes spreads her massive wings, dips down near the ground and then lands cleanly on my glove.

"There's my good Aggie girl," I say. Journee claps.

Now Mike blows his whistle. Squeal lets out a loud squawk and then dives down from the tree and onto Mike's glove. Now all three of the kids clap.

"Do it again," says Ayden.

I pull a dead white mouse of my pocket and feed it to Agnes as a reward. I toss one to Mike, and Squeal all but slurps it down.

"Okay, here we go," I say.

Mike and I move our arms and the raptors take off. Agnes and Squeal fly back and forth in a crisscross manner, like they are tying an invisible thread. Higher and higher they go. This time, they land in the same tree, with Agnes a few branches above Squeal.

"Look at her," I say. "Agnes always has to be the boss."

"C'mon, Agnes, get down here," I call and blow the whistle. Both birds return to our gloves and each gets a mouse. Mike and I fly them a little longer, but we have to be careful. If either of them feels full and is no longer hungry, then they could possibly refuse to come to the glove, or even fly away. The food is always the goal. They are predators, after all.

"Okay, one last time," I announce.

Squeal and Agnes take off from our gloves and fly up and in different directions, in a V-shape. Then they crisscross again and land on the same long branch at almost the same time.

Mike and I look at each other. He starts laughing, then I start laughing, then the kids start laughing. Journee even does some sort of halfway cartwheel.

This is what joy looks like. Suddenly I know that, somehow, Dippy's Dream is going to work out. I might not know how quite yet, but I know.

"Okay, y'all, let's get these birds back in their houses," I say. Mike and I call Agnes and Squeal back. They happily munch on dead white mice as our little group walks back to the aviaries.

"Ayden, Journee, Amina, which one of you is gonna be the next falconer in our family?" I ask them. They all raise their hands. "We'll be the family of Black falconers. Like the Jackson Five, but with birds."

Mike laughs at my lame joke.

"Seriously, though, Dad," he says. "Maybe as part of Dippy's Dream, we could give falconry classes and teach other Black people what they have to do to become master falconers if they want to."

I like that Mike has used the word *we*. That means he wants to be involved with Dippy's Dream in some way.

"That's a great idea, Goober," I say. "We could eventually start a Black falconers club, and part of it would be that the falconers donate some time volunteering at Dippy's Dream."

"Well, let's get the place built first, Dad."

We laugh, and Mike loads his kids up in the car.

"Bye, Pop Pop!" they call and wave.

I wave back and call, "Bye, baby birds!"

Chapter 14

January 2021

The year 2020 will likely go down in history as one of the most intense and tragic in modern history. For me, life was going well that year until the middle of March, when COVID-19 put the brakes on just about everything. Spring is usually the beginning of the busy season for Rodney's Raptors and ECC's Wings Over America, with multiple presentations at schools, nature centers, festivals, and the Laurel location. Those events were the first things to go. One after another—canceled or indefinitely postponed. ECC had to shut down all of its public programming. At Rodney's Raptors, I was getting texts and phone calls from people apologizing but canceling. I had to say no to one or two groups that still wanted to proceed; I just couldn't risk anyone getting sick, or me getting sick, either. Because I rely on funds from demonstrations and teaching gigs, my income dried up almost overnight.

I had a little bit of savings I had put away for Dippy's Dream, but I didn't want to dig into that. Even if I did, it wouldn't be enough to pay my bills and take care of my animals indefinitely. I had to apply for unemployment along with other ECC employees, and fortunately I was eligible. I would still be struggling, but at least I'd be able to feed myself, my birds, and my animals.

I regularly checked in on my family members and friends, making sure everyone was healthy and safe. Mike called to tell me that he and some of his co-workers at the fire station had tested positive for COVID-19 and that he wasn't feeling well. He had to quarantine for two weeks, and, perhaps because of his youth and good health, he recovered relatively quickly.

Another disappointment clocked in when the premiere of a documentary about my work was canceled. For the past several years, filmmaker Annie Kaempfer and her crew had been following me around, filming the work I do with raptors. The end result was accepted into the national Environmental Film Festival in Washington, DC. The premiere was supposed to take place in late March, but the entire festival had to go virtual. I was hoping the film would generate donations that would enable me to expand the work I was doing, but that didn't happen at the level I had hoped for.

By late spring, I knew I would have to recalibrate my efforts. My in-person gatherings with my raptors weren't going to resume anytime soon. I decided I would pivot and spend the extra time working on Dippy's Dream. I began driving to Virginia more frequently. I invested in a chainsaw and a wood chipper—still couldn't afford a tractor—and I started cutting down some of the trees. I would burn some of the wood and turn some of it into mulch. The process was exhausting and time-consuming, but by mid-summer I had cleared about 75 percent of the land that I would eventually use as the campground.

My birds and horses were still at the Laurel location, but my buddy Unk and I spent several days building the aviary in Virginia. On days when the weather was bad, I would work on designing the sign for Dippy's Dream that will eventually be placed at the front of my property. At least I could finally see progress being made.

Even though the impact of COVID-19 had stopped my work in its tracks, some positive things made me start to believe that this interruption wouldn't last forever. Annie's documentary, *The Falconer*, was accepted into several other film festivals, and even though they were virtual screenings, I knew the exposure would be good.

In early summer, I was contacted by an African American muralist named Mel Waters, who is based in

California. He was participating in an art project called Wide Open Walls, where artists and muralists promote diversity through artistic expression. Mel wanted to paint a huge mural of me holding Agnes on the wall of a building in Sacramento. I agreed, and he began to share with me the initial sketches.

As far as conservation and animal life is concerned, one good thing about the pandemic is that fewer people were driving on the highways and roads, and that meant that fewer raptors and deer would get hit and killed.

By late summer, it seemed that the country was more or less adjusting to the presence of COVID-19 and learning how to have safe, small, and socially distanced gatherings.

I started to get calls about being hired to bring some of my birds to small outdoor gatherings and celebrations, such as birthday parties. As long as all safety protocols were being followed, I jumped at the chance to have an income again.

In early fall, the Patuxent Research Refuge began to hold occasional outdoor nature demonstrations, mandating that visitors and presenters wear masks and stay socially distanced. Being outside, with the sun glittering off the water as I showed off Agnes and Mr. Hoots to eager young children, was something I wasn't sure could ever happen again. Even though it was fall, I felt like we were all coming back to life after a long, dark winter. Patuxent wasn't hosting weekly events like in the past, but even one or two a month was better than nothing.

Between the occasional but critical return of Rodney's Raptors to the public eye, working on Dippy's Dream, and caring for the raptors and animals, I had little time to worry about the future. That was never really my thing anyway—I'm more of a just-put-one-foot-in-front-of-the-other kind of guy.

Like most people, I couldn't wait to see 2020 come to an end. But November and December ended up being two important months in my life.

On November 25, my son Rodney Jr. and his girlfriend welcomed Rodney Vaughn Stotts III into the world. When I went to meet my namesake, I told his parents I'd have a falconer's glove on that child's hand by age three.

"Guess I'd better start building another aviary for the next Black falconer," I announced.

Around the same time, I received a phone call from a representative of the Mid-Atlantic Make-A-Wish organization. Their mission is to make dreams come true for critically ill children. They knew of a sick child whose dream was to be a falconer, and they wanted to know if I would give her a lesson.

For once in my life, I was speechless. I couldn't believe they had chosen me. I had seen stories about the organization connecting children with well-known or famous people to fulfill a dream, but I never imagined that falconry would be someone's dream and that I would be the one asked to fulfill it.

On a sunny day in mid-December, the nine-year-old girl arrived with her family and a person from Make-A-Wish. I taught her how to attach jesses to a raptor's ankles—Agnes was a willing participant—and how to feed the raptors. She learned how to wear the glove and let Agnes fly to it. That little lady was a born natural, and I told her so. I also told her that she was now a falconry apprentice and that I would be her sponsor.

When the last day of December came, I decided that we all needed some salvation from the brutal year we'd just gone through. I had just trapped a red-tailed hawk on my property, but because he was an adult, I would have to let him go. What if I released the hawk along with prayers and intentions? What would that look like? I posted on social media what I was going to do and asked people to send in their intentions. They came from far and wide:

"For my mother-in-law."

"For you, Rodney, and your program."

"For the Monacan Indian Nation."

"For Grandma."

"For all who lost loved ones this year."

"For the Chappaquiddick Tribe."

"For my wife's cousin who was in the military and just killed himself, and for his family."

"For 2021 to be better than 2020."

I scheduled a Facebook Live event and more than one hundred people tuned in.

The red-tailed hawk was contained in a carrier that I had placed in a clearing near the woods.

"Thank you all for sending in your prayer requests and intentions," I said to the viewers. "I am going to release them on the wings of this red-tailed hawk, along with some of my own. For Uncle Dexter, Aunt Faye, Grandma Lottie, Dippy, Chuck, Monique, Kareem, Wendell, Juwan, Uncle Mo, and Miss Betty. I was also asked to make an intention that people stop being mean. Honestly, 2020 has just got to go."

I bent over the carrier, untied the clasp, and opened the door. For a second, nothing happened, then the hawk took off, his brilliant tail feathers splayed wide.

"There you go," I said.

The hawk flew close to the ground to get his bearings, and then flapped his broad wings and climbed higher and higher, beyond the spindly trees, and away into the winter sky.

Acknowledgments

Special thanks to writer Kate Pipkin and to my agent Joy Tutela from the David Black Agency who enthusiastically believed in this project from its first inception. I also want to thank the dedicated team from Island Press including Courtney Lix, Sharis Simonian, Jaime Jennings, and Annie Byrnes.

I want to recognize the many people in my life who have shown me support and love during various times in my journey including Cornelius (Unk) Raynor; documentary filmmaker Annie Kaempfer; Mary L. (Weesie) Pipkin; and all those who have attended my presentations, and helped and supported me in the creation of Dippy's Dream. You know who you are.

Finally, I give all of my love and gratitude to my mother Mary (Dippy) Stotts and my brother Charles (Chuck) Alexander who made me the person I am today and without whom I would not be here, and to so many loved ones who no longer walk the Earth but who will remain in my heart and soul forever.

About the Authors

Raised in Southeast Washington, DC, Rodney Stotts has achieved the highest level of master falconer. Stotts is an educator and the founder and director of a successful educational nonprofit called Rodney's Raptors. When he's not on the sanctuary property located in Laurel, Maryland, Rodney lives on seven acres in Charlotte Court House, Virginia, where he is working to turn the property into a haven for underprivileged youth and anyone who is interested in learning about falconry, wildlife, and conservation. The finished project will be called Dippy's Dream, after Rodney's deceased mother. His work has been featured in *National Geographic*,

 National Public Radio, and other national outlets. He is the subject of the documentary film *The Falconer*.

Kate Pipkin is a writer and editor living and working in

Baltimore. She has contributed to the *Baltimore Sun*, *Baltimore Magazine*, *Johns Hopkins Magazine*, the *Loch Raven Review*, and other publications.

Image Credits

Photographs credited to Greg Kahn unless otherwise specified.

iii: Rodney holds Gloria, one of his Harris hawks.

vi: Gloria getting ready to take off and fly to Rodney's glove.

x: Rodney flying his beloved hawk, Agnes.

12: A portrait of Rodney outdoors, where he loves to be, in winter.

44: Rodney getting ready to give Agnes a mouse "treat" after she flies to his glove.

88: Rodney's son Mike teaching falconry basics to his stepson Aiden. Photo courtesy of Mike Jackson.

102: A portrait of Gloria landing on Rodney's glove.

136: Rodney shares a moment with Mr. Hoots, the Eurasian eagle-owl.

156: At a presentation in Southeast Washington, DC, Rodney encourages a child to touch Mr. Hoots' feathers.

198: Rodney talks to Mr. Hoots before a presentation.

208: Agnes devours a mouse Rodney has given her.